UNVEILED THREAT

A Personal Experience of Fundamentalist Islam and the Roots of Terrorism

Janet M. Tavakoli

To Stephen Kinzer,
I'm a long-time
admirer of your work!
With warm regards,
[illegible]
Nov. 24, 2014

Published by Lyons McNamara LLC, Chicago, Illinois.

Library of Congress Cataloging-in-Publication Data:

Tavakoli, Janet M.

Unveiled Threat / Janet M. Tavakoli

ISBN-10: 0985159057

ISBN-13: 978-0-9851590-5-4

Also by Janet Tavakoli

Non-fiction

Credit Derivatives & Synthetic Structures, 2nd Ed., John Wiley & Sons (1998, 2001).

Structured Finance & Collateralized Debt Obligations, 2nd Ed., John Wiley & Sons (2003, 2008).

Dear Mr. Buffett: What An Investor Learns 1,269 Miles from Wall Street, John Wiley & Sons (2009).

The New Robber Barons, Lyons McNamara LLC, 2012. (Compilation of chiefly web-based articles from the 2008 financial crisis to January 2012).

Fiction

Archangels: Rise of the Jesuits, Lyons McNamara LLC, January 2013. (Thriller)

Acknowledgements

I would like to thank the many people who contributed their comments and encouragement, especially Father J. Allan Meyer, Rita Ilse Guhrauer, Catharine A. Henningsen, Libby Fischer Hellmann, William J. Mikus, David Pelleg, and Diane Piron-Gelman.

Author's Note to Readers

This book represents my personal commentary based on my own experiences, interpretation of research, and observations. It is not meant to be a comprehensive analysis of the Middle East or fundamentalist Islam. Rather, it is an essay on my point of view. I present examples and explanations only to the extent I feel they are necessary to clarify my position.

You are reading the print edition. In the Kindle edition, I included hyperlinks to original sources. Internet links are subject to change or may disappear entirely without notice. The references for each chapter are also shown at the end of the Kindle book. In this print edition, I include reference numbers in superscript that correspond to references in the back, numbered in sequence by chapter, so that you can independently look up the source, if you so desire.

Arabic and Farsi, the national language of Iran, are both written in Arabic script. Over the years, English writers have used phonetic spelling, and there is no standard usage. Older readers may be accustomed to reading "Mohammed" for name of the prophet of Islam. In the past ten years or so, the mainstream press changed to Muhammad for the preferred spelling. Foreign words included in the Merriam-Webster English dictionary are not italicized, although there may be some discrepancy due to multiple accepted English spellings of the same word. The context should make the meaning clear.

Apostrophes are used to indicate glottal stops in many texts, but since this book is geared to native English speakers, I omit them. For example, for Islam's holy book, the Qur'an, I use Quran, formerly written in most Western works as Koran. When referring to Shi'ite Muslims, I usually use Shiite as an adjective and Shia as a noun, although even that isn't a hard and fast rule. I used the word that sounded most correct to me; usage is inconsistent even among Shias when speaking English.

To expect bad men never to do bad things is insensate; it is hoping for the impossible. To tolerate their offenses against others, and expect none against yourself, is both irrational and arbitrary.

—Marcus Aurelius

Contents

Preface

I am a fortunate woman. I was born in the United States to educated parents, attended private Catholic grammar and high schools, earned a B.S. in Chemical Engineering from the Illinois Institute of Technology, and earned an MBA in finance from the University of Chicago. Along the way I've learned to speak German, enough Japanese to get around, and a smattering of several other languages.

I've worked on Wall Street, and continue to have an interesting career in finance. The United States is a great place for women to thrive. Even when I clash with powerful men, no one threatens to kill me (not seriously, anyway).

No matter where I travel in the world, I'm happy to return home, where I am free to speak my mind and vote my preferences. I was never happier than when I returned from Iran after living there during the year of the revolution that birthed the Islamic Republic of Iran in 1979.

For decades I've studied the saga of the roots of fundamentalist Islamic terrorism and watched the movement grow. After terrorism came to New York while I lived there, I realized I never really got completely away.

In September 2014, His Excellency Iyad bin Amin Madani, Secretary General of the Organization of Islamic Cooperation (OIC), addressed an assembly of the Chicago Council on Global Affairs. The OIC states it is a political, not a religious, organization and includes fifty-seven countries.

I asked him why criminals from so many different countries and cultures continue to band together in the name of Islam and commit mayhem and murder authorized by the highest levels of Islamic clergy. Some of these are political acts designed to bring down other countries.

He dodged the question.

If he had answered, my follow-up question would have been, "Why have so many Islamic countries institutionalized intolerance for other religions and sanctioned abuse of women?"

This book represents my own perspective on the answers to these questions based on my personal experiences and observations.

Chapter 1

Iran: The White Revolution

No Country in the World Has a Worse Record on Human Rights

—Amnesty International on Iran, 1974

In the summer of 1978, Mohammed Reza Pahlavi was the Shah of Iran. The iron curtain was still drawn, and Jimmy Carter was President of the United States. *Animal House* opened in U.S. movie theaters. Bonnie Tyler's *It's a Heartache* and Abba's *Take a Chance on Me* were at the top of the pop charts.

Poor Men Want to be Rich

When I arrived in Tehran, the palpable excitement of the upwardly mobile city hit me like a blast of hot dry air. Iranians enthusiastically embraced consumerism as the oil revenue-fueled economy flourished.

When I first walked down Pahlavi Street in 1978, young adults pored over foreign magazines at local newsstands. Jeans made in the USA were prized possessions.

The Shah's father had already eliminated the requirement that women wear the chador, a sheet-like cloak worn over the head and clutched under the chin. Only around one of every six women wore it anymore, either out of modesty, religious belief, family pressure, or an ulterior motive. My brother-in-law pointed out a chador-clad local prostitute. He claimed prostitutes wore the chador as camouflage.

Most women wore European and American clothes. Women matched jeans with high heels, expensive silk shirts, ropes of gold, and diamond earrings. Some wore expensive Italian or Parisian outfits. They skillfully enhanced their beautiful features with black eyeliner and red lipstick and sported elegantly coiffed hair.

Everyone with a bike wanted a motorbike, everyone with a motorbike wanted an Iranian-made Paykan automobile, and everyone with a Paykan wanted a sleek foreign sports car. Wealthy Iranians sent their children to study at prestigious schools in the United States, France, Switzerland, England, and Germany. Ambitious men brought home foreign wives.

The Shah had declared a bloodless White Revolution in 1963 with twelve social and economic reforms, including land reform, women's rights, and battling illiteracy among the lower classes. By the mid-1970's, his drawing board held grandiose plans: dozens of new military schemes, the reconstruction of Tehran with a gigantic plaza in his honor, the world's most opulent subway, and national industrialization. The Shah needed every penny of oil revenues, and he was determined to protect his assets.

Iran's military complex boomed. The U.S. military trained Iranian troops. A naval station at Bandar Abbas protected the mouth of the Persian Gulf. The Shah's military protected Kharg Island, once famous for pearls, and then the site of one of the world's largest offshore oil terminals. (Iraq bombed it during the Iran-Iraq War in the 1980s.) The Shah had given generous military aid to Oman to fight the Dhofar rebels and was the go-to source for military support in the region.

The Shah expanded industries and built utility plants. For the first time, electric lights illuminated small villages, and the new middle class installed telephones. Waves of foreign businessmen flooded into the country and rented homes.

Iran's economy was growing fast, and Tehran, its largest city, was the heart of the blossoming country. Iranians called it the Paris of the Middle East, a playground for the prosperous.

Rich Men Want to Be Kings

The Shah seemed to be a champion of women's rights. He had three wives, but not at the same time. He was a serial monogamist.

In 1939, he married Fawzia Fuad, the stunning blue-eyed daughter of King Fuad I of Egypt. Within ten years she divorced him and returned to Egypt with their daughter.

In 1951, he married Soraya Esfandiary, a mercurial green-eyed half-German, half-Iranian beauty. The Shah, still a puppet of the United States, partied and skied with his new wife in Cannes, Paris, London, Gstaad, Zermatt, and St. Moritz. Soraya was unable to have children, so he divorced her in 1958. The Shah was pushing forty, and his 33-year-old so-called dynasty needed a male heir.

In 1959 he married 21-year-old Farah Diba. Ten months later she had a son, followed by three more children, including another son. (The youngest daughter committed suicide in London in 2001, and the youngest son committed suicide in Boston in 2011.)

The Shah did advance women's rights, up to a point. He introduced women's suffrage. Women served in the Iranian army, received six months training, and taught villagers to read and write as part of his plan to reduce Iran's 75% illiteracy rate. Yet polygamy was still allowed providing two conditions were met: the first wife had to agree, and the court had to approve.

The façade sparkled with promise, but when you looked inside you saw a wreck. The Shah was a misogynist. In an interview with journalist Oriana Falacci, he denigrated women's abilities and asserted, "Women count only if they're beautiful and graceful and know how to stay feminine." In the same interview he blurted, "You're schemers, you're evil. Every one of you."

Kings Want to Be Gods

Mohammad Reza Pahlavi claimed he ruled by divine right, and his authority came from the will of Allah. He called himself an Emperor, a King of Kings. It was an extraordinary claim from a man who sometimes didn't have enough to eat as a child and whose father was a commoner.

He claimed he had visions from God and that the long-dead first Imam Ali saved him from a nasty fall when he was a child. In a 1974 cover story, *Time* quoted William Simon, then U.S. Secretary of the Treasury, characterizing the Shah as "an irresponsible and reckless…nut."[1]

Simon's animosity had nothing to do with the Shah's self-proclaimed visions. In 1973 the Arab oil embargo quadrupled oil prices. After the Saudis took all the risk, and only after it was clear the West wouldn't launch a military intervention, the Shah appointed himself spokesman for the new Organization of Petroleum Exporting Countries (OPEC) cartel.

The Shah couldn't conceive of an end to his brand new hereditary monarchy. He often said that the people respected him as if he were their father. Educated Iranians laughed in disbelief.

Mohammad Reza Pahlavi's own father, Reza Khan, a member of the Persian Cossack Brigade, deposed Ahmad Shah Qajar, head of the 140-year-old Qajar dynasty, in 1925. Reza Khan was a poor but ambitious army officer. Through craftiness and ruthlessness, the crude thuggish man stole a crown.

During a meeting with a Greek dignitary, a Mr. Kyriakos, pronounced "kir ya kos," Reza Khan made a joke true to his peasant upbringing. *Kir* and *kos* are names for male and female genitalia in Farsi. *Ya* means or. Reza Khan taunted his diplomatic guest by asking him to make up his mind. What was he? Kir or kos?

His son, Shah Mohammed Reza Pahlavi, was educated in Europe and dressed either in expensive bespoke suits or military dress festooned with unearned medals. He spoke French and German better than he spoke Farsi. Upper-class Iranians considered him an interloper. He was an insecure common bully who never saw a day of combat, a man who made others do his dirty work.

The Shah's thugs kept dissenters in line. My uncle-in-law had once owned a major news publication in Iran. He published a political cartoon depicting the Shah's second wife, Soraya, riding him like a donkey. The Shah had him imprisoned and destroyed his printing operation. When he was released from prison, he abandoned publishing and lived a comfortable, but idle compromise of a life.

With the help of Israel's Mossad and General Schwartzkopf's father, the Shah formed SAVAK, a brutal secret service agency that specialized in censorship, surveillance, torture, and execution. Iranians studying at foreign universities were cautious and often suspected their fellow Iranian students were spies for SAVAK, because of the Shah's massive investment in surveillance.

The large class divide, grand ambitions of the insecure Shah, discontent among religious leaders, brutality of the dictatorship, and, crucially, an old grudge against the United States, were about to spark a revolution.

Coup d'état: CIA, MI6 and Mossadegh

Why did Iranians hold a grudge against the United States?

In April 1951, the Shah appointed Prime Minister Mohammad Mossadegh, after Iran's Majles, a democratically elected parliament, voted for Mossadegh with an overwhelming majority. The United States and Britain drove Mossadegh out of power to support the then-powerless Shah.

A month after Mossadegh rose to power, Iran nationalized the Anglo-Iranian Oil Company and renamed it the National Iranian Oil Company. Mossadegh wanted a fair share of the profits and higher pay for Iranian workers who lived in hovels and earned a fraction of the pay of their British counterparts. Mossadegh took a hard line, boycotted the British, and cut diplomatic ties. It was the beginning of the end of his career. He hurt Iran's revenues and riled both Britain and the United States.

After exercising his constitutional right to control the military, Mossadegh asked the parliament for emergency powers, and he got them. He stripped the Shah of as much power and access to money as he could, and expelled the Shah's politically active twin sister, Ashraf. The shaken Shah fled to Europe.

Britain wasn't about to let its control of Iranian oil go without a fight, and the Eisenhower Administration didn't like Mossadegh's policies any more than Britain.

Allen Dulles headed the Central Intelligence Agency (CIA); his brother, John Foster Dulles, was Secretary of State. The Dulles brothers had been lawyers with the Wall Street law firm of Sullivan and Cromwell, and one of the firm's clients was the British Anglo-Iranian Oil Company—now known as British Petroleum, or BP.

Why did the United States get involved? What was good for American oil companies was good for America. Oil is a global commodity and the price of oil depends on the marginal cost of production per barrel. Iran could have a lot of influence in driving up global oil prices.

The United States and Great Britain launched Operation Ajax, a joint covert military operation designed to get rid of Mossadegh. Kermit Roosevelt, son of former President Theodore Roosevelt, helped with logistics and payoffs. After the first coup d'état attempt failed, the CIA paid local Iranians to instigate riots in the streets of Tehran. More than 300 Iranians were killed, and many more were wounded. CIA operatives posed as communists and engineered the bombing of a mullah's home to sour the Muslim religious community against Mossadegh's secular democracy.[2]

The CIA must wax nostalgic over how cheaply people could be bought. According to Steven Kinzer's *All the Shah's Men*, the British gave Ashraf Pahlavi $10,000 and a mink coat to persuade her craven twin brother, who was hiding out in Rome, to sign royal orders to oust Mossadegh.[3]

The coup d'état finally succeeded. At the end of August 1953, Mossadegh was out, and the Shah was in. We got our way.

In 2000, Dr. Madeleine Albright, then U.S. Secretary of State in President Clinton's administration, acknowledged America made mistakes in Iran, including the role we played in the 1953 coup that restored Shah Mohammad Reza Pahlavi's power.[4]

In 2013, the *National Security Archive*[5] published a declassified CIA document acknowledging its complicity:[6]

> The military coup that overthrew Mosadeq [alternate spelling of Mossadegh] and his National Front cabinet was carried out under CIA direction as an act of U.S. foreign policy, conceived and approved at the highest levels of government.

It took 60 years for the CIA to declassify the documents.

The Shah and Ayatollah Khomeini's Fatwa

Once Mossadegh was ousted, the Shah returned to the Peacock Throne. Through a system of gifts, bribes, consulting fees, and partnerships in major business deals, the Pahlavis rose from a family that could barely feed itself in the 1930s to one of the wealthiest families in the world. It was a remarkable feat since the Shah's only calluses were those on the fingers that held the reins of the horses he loved to ride.

The Shah's biggest mistake was that he didn't give Islamic religious leaders a cut of the swag. Mullahs felt they weren't getting their fair share of corruption, power, and profits.

Ayatollah Ruhollah Mousavi Khomeini was a deeply damaged man. He was born in 1902 in

Khomein. His father died when he was two, and when he was only sixteen, both his mother and a cherished aunt died. He threw himself into the role of the Islamic holy man, using his authority to act as a cruel despot. By the time he was in his fifties, his influence had grown, and he joined a nationwide campaign against the peaceful followers of the Bahai faith.

In 1962, the Shah tried to eliminate the requirement that elected local officials be sworn in on the Quran. The Shah's idea was that the official could choose his religious text. Khomeini interpreted this as sympathy for the Bahai faith, and demanded the Shah stop violating the law of Islam. Muslims boycotted and protested, and the Shah rescinded the order. Khomeini got his first taste of real power.

When the Shah announced his White Revolution in 1963, Khomeini resisted the Shah's social reforms, issued a fatwa, and denounced the Shah as a puppet of Israel and America.

The Shah retaliated by marching with troops to the city of Qom, Khomeini's home, and attacking religious scholars in a scathing speech. When Khomeini lashed back, the Shah transported him to Tehran's infamous Qasr prison.

News of Khomeini's incarceration spread through Iran and his supporters rioted for six days. The Shah's troops finally quelled the uproar and eventually allowed Khomeini to return to Qom in the spring of 1964.

In the fall of that year, the Shah agreed to give American personnel and their dependents immunity from prosecution. Khomeini denounced the move and called the Shah a sell-out.

The Shah's troops escorted Khomeini to Tehran's airport and gave him a one-way ticket to Turkey. From there Khomeini fled to Iraq and spent thirteen years encouraging people to strike and revolt against the Shah's government. In a style later adopted by Osama bin-Laden, Khomeini made radio broadcasts, and his supporters smuggled cassettes into Iran to spread the word throughout the country.

Meanwhile, the Shah tried to liberate women in villages from the veil. It was a good idea, in theory, but he was a despot and his methods showed it. Armed soldiers marched into villages and snatched chadors off defenseless women. Have you ever met anyone who felt liberated by invading bullies? Village women were caught in the middle, between men who abused them in the street for wearing the chador and men who abused them when they got home for not wearing the chador.

The Shah also jailed and tortured dissidents, including members of the press. People were held without counsel, without access to communication, and without trial. In 1974 Amnesty International asserted Iran had the worst human rights record of any country in the world. The United States pressured the Shah to improve human rights and to allow freedom of the press.

In response, the Shah relaxed controls. Illiterate old men stood on street corners listening to literate young men read the criticisms of the Shah that *Ettalat*, Iran's major newspaper, now dared to write.

In 1978 Khomeini moved to Neauphle-le-Château, a suburb of Paris, where he gave interviews to the international press and denounced the Shah. In August, Khomeini's supporters barred exits of a movie theater in Abadan, set it on fire, and killed 477 people. Bodies were piled inside the doors, evidence of the futility of the victims' attempts to escape. The terrorists fled to Iraq, but pinned the blame on SAVAK.

Riots broke out throughout Iran.

"Death to the Shah! Death to America!"

By November of 1978, foreigners stopped talking about the weather and instead asked about the anarchy factor. One late fall day, I opened the door of the heavy gate to our high-walled garden as students fled the Shah's advancing troops. I ventured out into the street, wishing I had my camera. More students rounded the corner with four soldiers hot on their heels.

The soldiers weren't taking aim through the sights of their rifles; they simply fired in the direction of the running students. Several students clutched wounds as they streamed by.

A young man shoved me back into the garden and shouted: "Lady, they are going to shoot you; they think you are a student!" He was right. I was wearing jeans. Two other students darted inside and helped me shut and secure the garden door. They said that the Shah's troops daily broke up demonstrations and denied the right of free assembly. The students waited a couple of hours, and when they were sure the street was clear of soldiers, they exited the garden and disappeared.

The Shah imposed military curfews, but they were unpredictable. One night the curfew would be 9:00; the next night it could be 11:00; the next night it could be sundown. The arbitrary curfews had people confused, and Iranians who attended parties and then returned home risked arrest.

If you were found on the street without identification, you were immediately arrested. If you had identification, you might be able to talk and bribe your way out of being detained, if you were lucky. Foreigners were openly harassed and physically attacked throughout the city.

The troops patrolling Tehran were from the provinces, since it was thought that soldiers would not be willing to fire on people from their home towns. Even with this precaution, defections were a daily occurrence. Soon it was hard to tell whether soldiers still worked for the Shah or whether they sided with the revolution.

One evening the Shah's armed troops stormed into my ballet lesson at the American Women's Club. They claimed there were rumors fundamentalists planned an attack on the club. The soldiers stood in the doorway of the dance class leering at us. They seemed to want to intimidate us into leaving. They continued to watch as we threw our clothes over our leotards. I looked out the window to see more troops in a truck on the street outside. No fundamentalists bothered the club that night.

Foreign women married to Iranians could not leave the country without the permission of their husbands, and some husbands controlled them by refusing it. Women lined up outside their embassies hoping for help, but their embassies could do nothing. The women were subject to Iranian law.

Bell Helicopter employees received death threats delivered via fax machines. Employees arrived at work to find more death threats on their desks. Foreign company officers received phone calls with bomb threats. Protesters fire-bombed buses transporting foreign workers.

I knew a British couple, Rupert and Katherine, who were near retirement age. They had agreed to an assignment in Iran, because it paid a premium. Katherine called me around 11:00 one cold night. She had heard about several bombings that day, and her husband hadn't come home. She couldn't reach anyone where he worked, and she was frantic.

Rupert was on one of the buses that was bombed. Several of his colleagues were killed or injured. Rupert was stunned from the blast, and bleeding from a head wound. When a group of Iranian men surrounded the bus and shouted: "Death to Americans!", he realized the crowd posed a threat and escaped the bus to continue the journey on foot. Several of the young men followed him, occasionally hitting him, sometimes shoving him, and constantly taunting him.

Rupert walked the streets of the city for eight hours hoping his tormentors would tire and give up on him. He was afraid to return home, since the rabble would know where he lived, and Katherine was alone in the apartment during the day. He finally shook them and returned home around 1:00 am.

Within a week or two, foreign companies pulled out all non-essential personnel.

The Shah's troops tried to quell widespread resistance in Tehran. Rumors flew that soldiers shot 10,000 people in Jaleh Square, one of the plazas in the southern part of the city. The army cut off the exits, and the infantry shot straight at the demonstrators. They were assisted by soldiers in helicopters who shot downward into the crowd.

The Shah's news flacks retorted that only 5,000 people were in the square, and only a few dozen people had been killed—as if that made the Shah's actions reasonable.

The sound of low-flying helicopters constantly filled the air. Calm neighborhoods turned suddenly dangerous as crushing waves of protesters shouted: "Death to the Shah! Death to America! Americans are the Devil!"

One day my ex-brother-in-law and I were waiting in a long line for Melli bank to open its doors. We heard distant angry voices. The shouting grew louder and closer. My brother-in-law gave me the keys to his American-made, large cream-colored Oldsmobile and told me to drive away as fast as I could. If the crowd discovered that I was an American, he couldn't protect me.

But driving away might not have been safe, either. Cars were pounded and overturned with passengers still inside. Sometimes the drivers were dragged from their cars and beaten, after which their cars were torched.

My brother-in-law refused to go with me; he wanted to stay and see for himself what would happen next. As I got in the car and drove off, the shouts became a roar. Hundreds of rioters poured into the street. I knew the Shah's troops wouldn't be far behind, and they would have orders to shoot into rioting crowds.

I traveled about a half mile and found myself in the midst of another rioting crowd. Three men circled the car and peered at me through the glass. Suddenly something diverted their attention, and they walked swiftly away. I drove around other cars and after several illegal maneuvers, got into a clear lane and made a beeline for home.

An hour later my sister-in-law arrived home, hysterical and crying. She was Iranian, but had lightened her hair and looked American. A group of angry men had pounded on her window shouting anti-American slogans, and threatened to overturn her car with her in it.

Khomeini, who was still in France, courted the European press and called for general strikes.

Iran ground to a halt. Gasoline, fuel oil to heat homes, and food staples were difficult to find except at black market prices. Iranians normally bought bread hot from the baker's oven, and shortages of wheat flour caused shortages at bakeries. Quarter mile lines formed as customers waited for a single loaf of bread. People asked around, wondering which bakeries might open and have bread that day.

Waves of electrical brown-outs hit the city. Electricity went out for twelve hours at a time, always unannounced, always random. Refrigerators weren't up to the task and food spoiled. People began buying deep freezers to keep food, but there weren't enough to go around for any price, and the poor couldn't afford them. Popular brands disappeared from food store shelves as people began hoarding, and new supplies failed to arrive.

The balance of power was shifting from the Shah to armed revolutionaries. When Khomeini sent word to Iran that he was returning, the military responded by closing Tehran airport.

In the months before the Shah lost power, the Shah filled the prisons. Government opportunists demanded ransoms. In December 1978, two of the men who worked for Ross Perot's EDS Corporation were taken hostage in Tehran and thrown into Qasr prison. The extortion price for their release was set at $12,750,000.

The government was in chaos. The Shah's brutal tactics weren't enough to keep control of the city. Most Iranians welcomed the revolution, even if it meant an Islamic Republic under a new megalomaniac.

Chapter 2

Islamic Republic: Descent into Darkness

The most painful state of being is remembering the future, especially one you can never have.

—Kierkegaard

I am now convinced that the worst thing that can happen to any country is to allow Islamic fundamentalists to have a say in government.

On January 16, 1979, the Shah fled Iran for the second—and last—time. He wouldn't return. On February 1, the Iranian Islamic Revolution welcomed back Ayatollah Khomeini. Many already called him imam, head of Iran's majority Shiite branch of Islam. Khomeini didn't fit the criteria to become an imam; he wasn't a direct descendant of Muhammad through his grandsons, Hasan and Husayn, but that didn't seem to matter. His supporters had most of the guns.

Friction between the small minority of Iranians that belonged to the Sunni Muslim sect and the overwhelming majority of Shiite Muslims festered beneath the surface. The Sunni Muslims were worried.

I was worried, too. Technically, I was a citizen of both Iran and the United States; a foreign woman married to an Iranian man got an Iranian passport almost as soon as the foreign marriage was recorded. But I am decidedly a blue-eyed American, and anyone who put a bullet in my head would score 100 points.

Khomeini delivered his first speech at the Tehran cemetery, Behesht-e Zahra. He denounced the Shah and called the United States "The Great Satan." Khomeini would soon fill all the cemeteries with bodies, then build new cemeteries and fill them with corpses, too.

People poured into the streets yelling, *"Death to the Shah! Death to America! Hail to Khomeini!"* More riots broke out; everyone waved guns in the air and sometimes shot off a few rounds.

The military fought amongst themselves. Young Air Force cadets warred with the Imperial Guard. The number of dead was rumored to be between five and five hundred. Emotions ran high and no one could tell what was rumor or truth.

Citizens in major cities rioted and openly defied the military curfew. Then the army slapped an early afternoon curfew on the major cities. Khomeini told his supporters to ignore it. Fighting and rioting continued, but the army didn't have the will to kill or arrest Khomeini's supporters. They returned to their barracks on the morning of February 10, and avoided what would probably have been a long bloody battle. By February 11, 1979, Khomeini was in power.

The revolution created an opportunity for Ross Perot. (Perot later made a failed bid for the U.S. presidency.) He personally organized and funded a strike team to extract his men. Perot hired retired Green Beret Colonel Bull Simon, who recruited and trained Perot's corporate employees.

Amidst the turmoil, Perot flew into Tehran airport himself, visited his men in prison, and managed to get out of the country after his men impressed upon him the precariousness of his situation. They were right. Had he stayed, Perot would have been executed and ended up another corpse in the courtyard of Qasr prison.

The events of February 11 were a stroke of luck for Perot's strike team. While they were casing the prison and formulating the escape plan, revolutionary forces stormed the building and released all the Shah's prisoners.

Perot's dream team provided the weakened prisoners with documents, cash, medical help, food, transportation, moral support, and protection. They drove overland past dangerous and unpredictable regional militias, braved through checkpoints, and crossed the border into Turkey. Then they drove through Turkey's bandit-ridden "blood alley," in the opposite direction from the one my husband and I took when we drove into Iran. Ken Follett immortalized the escape in his 1983 non-fiction thriller, *On Wings of Eagles*.[1]

Throughout Iran, sycophants flattered Khomeini just as a former group of bootlickers had flattered the Shah. Mullahs claimed they saw Khomeini's face in the full moon. Merchants swapped their ubiquitous photographs of the Shah with a photo of Khomeini.

On February 16, 1979, Iran's corrupt court system passed death sentences on four of the Shah's former generals. They were taken to the roof of Khomeini's headquarters in Tehran, lined up in front of a firing squad, and shot. It was just the beginning.

Khomeini banned liquor, drugs, and pornography. Anyone caught at the airports smuggling in contraband was immediately arrested.

Revolutionary forces took over the radio and television stations. Khomeini's followers fired most of the female newscasters. Their replacements covered their hair and wore bulky clothing that covered everything except their make-up free faces and hands. Broadcasts became a bland nasal singsong of praise for the revolutionaries, praise for Khomeini, criticism of the Shah, and criticism of the West: the mantra of the dreary Islamic theocratic utopia.

Khomeini banished joy from the airwaves. *Little House on the Prairie* was still allowed. The actresses dressed modestly and had few opportunities outside the home. Poor rural America from 100 years ago made Iran look less backward.

During the Shah's reign, television stations broadcast entertainment: Persian variety shows and dubbed foreign television programs. Iranians were famous for their love of music and dancing. They launched debates at the top of their lungs. Silly jokes were a part of everyday life. Now they entertained themselves behind closed doors with their curtains drawn.

The country assumed the appearance of the grim Iron Curtain countries I had driven through to reach Iran. All of the energy and light had been sucked into an Islamic black hole.

A nationwide referendum transformed Iran at the end of March. The people of Iran voted in Ayatollah Khomeini as their Supreme Leader, and supreme leaders have no term limits. Iranian presidents come and go, but the supreme leader has concentrated power and pulls all the strings.

Khomeini stuffed the parliament with a motley crew of mullahs and called it "Allah's government."

Pahlavi had failed to convince anyone he ruled by divine right, but Khomeini succeeded with a significant chunk of the Iranian population. It wasn't enough for him to overthrow the Shah; it wasn't enough for him to be supreme leader, Khomeini claimed his interpretation of Islam was the last word, because he was an imam appointed by Allah.

Khomeini was even crazier than the Shah. But if you laughed about it in Iran, you were very likely to get a fatal beating or risk getting your head shot off.

The provinces outside Tehran knew that life under Khomeini's rule would be much worse than life under the Shah's rule. Khuzestan, once part of the Arab Homeland, rebelled first. They demanded a greater share of the oil revenues and more jobs for the locals. Khomeini quelled the rebellion by shooting demonstrators and arresting their Shiite religious leader, Arabic-speaking Ayatollah Shubayr al Khaqani. He died suspiciously in 1986 while under house arrest.

Next the Kurds demanded autonomy. Khomeini broke his promise to never use the army against the Iranian people when he sent the military to quell the Kurdish rebellion.

Islamic Rule: Vengeance, Greed, and Crimes against Humanity

Khomeini had finally achieved the pinnacle of his ambition, and his stewardship was worse on every level than the injustices for which he had criticized the Shah.

Khomeini immediately destroyed Iran's civil rights. Women lost all their gains. Religious tolerance disappeared. Rule of law was demolished. Khomeini initiated a program of torture and summary executions.

Khomeini authorized "revolutionary courts." Mullahs led kangaroo courts called *komitehs*, and used changeable interpretations of sharia, Islamic law, to mete out punishments.

Neighbor turned on neighbor. Envious people denounced more successful ones who had prospered under the Shah. People were accused, dragged out of their stately homes in the middle of the night, and executed. Shortly thereafter, mullahs took up residence in their abandoned mansions.

Mullahs televised the important trials. The charges were always vague and the so-called evidence was a hash of unsubstantiated allegations. The accused were not allowed to defend themselves. Mullahs, some of whom were illiterate, presided together. The mullahs charged prisoners with "crimes against the Revolution."

Trials followed a pattern. An obviously abused prisoner was brought into a room, sparsely furnished with a long rectangular table and a few chairs, to hear the judgment of the mullahs. The prisoner could not defend himself. Questions were framed as accusations. When a prisoner tried to respond, the mullahs shouted him down and browbeat him. The prisoner was pronounced guilty. The sentence was death.

The next morning, the front page of the newspapers showed a picture of the bodies of hapless prisoners executed after the previous evening's trials. Men lay on their backs, naked from the waist up.

The stream of executions included Imperial Army officers, police officers, people rumored to be SAVAK agents, heads of families connected to the Shah, prominent businessmen, cabinet ministers, members of the *Majlis* (parliament), military officers, and former prime ministers. There were criminals among them, but that was no excuse for the absence of a fair trial. Moreover, some of the defendants were completely innocent of any crime, but their wealth and notoriety had attracted the greed of the new corrupt regime.

Iran became a nation of medieval witch hunts and arbitrary executions. There was no due process, no rule of rational law.

Since these bloodthirsty madmen craved a television audience, they had no deniability. Every Islamic cleric knew what was going on.

Acts of minor terrorism riddled the country. One of my father-in-law's workers was killed in a bomb explosion when he was delivering goods. No one ever found out why he was killed, or even if he was the intended target.

Khomeini's agenda never included rebuilding Iran to make it a better place to live for the average citizen. Citizens could wait until death to get their rewards. Men who were Islamic martyrs would be served in paradise by houris, dark-eyed female virgins who would bring them food and drink.

The Shah had modified Iran's culture, but Khomeini destroyed it with bitter determination. Iran's literacy rate had improved dramatically under the Shah; under Khomeini, it rapidly regressed.

In the madrasas, the religious schools, boys sat in rows in front of a mullah. They had no books, no pens, and no paper. The boys learned to recite the Quran in Arabic, even though they didn't understand most of the language. Mullahs can be illiterate as long as they study the Quran, Islamic traditions, and sharia law. Much of Islam is passed down via oral tradition.

The mullahs also preached hate against Americans, propaganda about how women should behave, and obedience to the government controlled by Islamic clerics.

Iranians took on a siege mentality. As one man explained, in Iran it was us against them: "My country against your country, my tribe against your tribe, cousin against cousin, and finally brother against brother, until there is no fighting left to be done."

People closed ranks and were unwilling to share their plans or to trust anyone. Many panicked.

When Money Dies

The official exchange rate was seven *toman* to the U.S. dollar, but after Khomeini returned, there were no means to convert money. Banks were closed much of the time. The government enacted restrictions. Iranians could convert the equivalent of $1,000 in U.S. currency and take it out of the country. Persian carpets were labeled national protected works of art, and the new government slapped an export ban on them.

Desperate people turned to the black market, but there were harsh punishments for anyone caught exchanging money.

Land and housing values plummeted to almost zero in the revolution's aftermath. Iranians with foreign bank accounts picked up screaming bargains from sellers who needed hard currency.

Travelers were only allowed one suitcase of clothing. Iranians bought diamonds and precious gemstones in secret from private citizens. These small valuable items could be concealed as portable currency, if they were able to flee the country. Families traded land, Persian carpets, and mansions for hand-carried, concealable wealth.

The luckiest Iranians already owned foreign homes, had large overseas bank balances, and owned businesses in foreign countries. Their children were already studying abroad. Many had fled even before the Shah did.

In March 1979, arrests began to crescendo. Families that had been close to the Shah were targets. One evening a family friend, whose father had been a supporter of the Shah, pleaded with my brother-in-law for help. Her father had been arrested. She asked everyone to use their influence, or he would be tortured and probably killed. I never learned his final fate.

Some of the wealthiest Iranians overstayed their welcome. They were arrested and executed, and all of their wealth was stolen by the new regime.

The infrastructure was breaking down. Production at the Tehran refinery dropped to one-quarter of its capacity, down from 85-90% of production capacity under the Shah. Khomeini knew how to destroy, but he didn't know how to build.

No Country for a Free Woman

How did Iran revert so quickly from an emerging modern society to the dark ages?

The only organized resistance came from the Shah's loyalists, most of whom were arrested and executed. Some of us objected on humanitarian grounds, but we weren't organized, and no one wanted to be the first to publicly object.

In game theory, this is called the Volunteer Game, and it is a game no one wants to play alone. In Joseph Heller's novel *Catch-22*, Yossarian balks at flying a suicide mission. When his superior officer asks, "What if everyone felt that way?" Yossarian answers, "Then I'd be a damned fool to feel any other way. Wouldn't I?"

The same was true in Iran. Moderate Iranians didn't put up a fight. It was inconceivable to them that anything that came next would be worse than the Shah. By the time they realized the full horror of what was happening under Khomeini, it was too late. Some fled, some got on board, and others acquiesced to it by silence.

The country was swept up in revolutionary rhetoric backed by armed force. At first, my husband thought Khomeini would oust the Shah and then step aside for a democratically elected government. Boy, was he wrong. Iran became no place for Americans, and it became no place for a free woman. It was time to leave, but my husband made excuses.

When we had lived in the United States, and when we first moved to Iran, I was an asset. He got a green card in America, and in the Iranian community, an American wife was a status symbol. But now the United States was unpopular. My husband said that he should go to parties without me, because some people disliked Americans. In June 1979, with only a suitcase of clothes and $1,000, I returned to the United States and divorced him. My belongings and money stayed in Iran. I felt as if I had paid my own ransom and was grateful to be back in the USA, the land of opportunity.

Iran's Islamic Republic of Fanaticism

Khomeini consolidated power and was eager to see the Shah dead. In October 1979, he flew into a rage when the Shah sought treatment for cancer in the United States.

In November of 1979, "student radicals" backed by Khomeini rushed the U.S. embassy and took the ninety people inside hostage. Some were released, but fifty-two remained hostages while Jimmy Carter dithered throughout a 444-day long crisis.

Carter didn't support the Shah, and the Pahlavi family left for Panama in December. When Iran petitioned Panama for extradition, the Shah sought asylum with Anwar el-Sadat in Egypt.

It didn't matter that the Shah had left the United States. Iran still held the American hostages. Carter halted Iranian oil imports and froze Iranian assets in the U.S. He also tried diplomatic solutions. Then five months into the crisis, in April of 1980, Carter tried a military rescue.

Carter's extraction attempt failed. The U.S. military had misjudged the ability of the rescue helicopters to handle desert sandstorms. Eight Americans died, and three of the eight helicopters were damaged.

The Shah died in Egypt in July 1980, and Iran resumed negotiations with the United States. As President Ronald Reagan was being sworn in on January 20, 1981, Iran released the hostages, and the United States thawed the freeze of around $8 billion in Iranian assets.

In September 1980, Iraq invaded Iran. Khomeini sent men to war. He also sent untrained prepubescent boys into bloody battles, instead of to school. He told parents their virgin children would be martyrs and find their reward in paradise.

The formal bitter conflict lasted eight years and cost 500,000 lives. Both Iran and Iraq stunted education, neglected the maintenance—much less the improvement—of their countries' infrastructures, and wasted the energies of their nations in hatred of their enemies.

Khomeini was at war with the non-Islamic world and with a large swath of the non-Shia Islamic world. Freedom of speech and international law were alien concepts. He also lacked a sense of humor. His son once told a reporter he had never seen him laugh. Khomeini died of prostate cancer in June of 1989, and Ayatollah Ali Khamenei became Iran's new supreme leader.

Today, through the Imam Reza Foundation,[2] Muslim clerics control the largest chunk of Iran's wealth. The martyrs' shrine in Mashhad annually draws an estimated 12 to 20 million people, who contribute to the foundation. The foundation has a huge portfolio of corporations and business interests, including confiscated wealth. The National Iranian Oil Company is Iran's second largest business enterprise. The Iranian Revolutionary Guard Corps (IRGC) became an industry of their own, and they are the third largest business enterprise. Estimates of the size of the IRGC's Quds Force (aka Qods), Iranian Special Operations reporting directly to the supreme leader, range from 2,000 to 15,000.

Informal conflict with Iraq is ongoing. In 2004, Iranian assassins, possibly members of the Quds, used the United States' invasion to infiltrate Iraq and systematically hunt down and murder Sunni Iraqi pilots who bombed Iran during the Iran-Iraq War sixteen years earlier.[3]

Khamenei and his henchmen practiced the same brand of militant Islam as Khomeini, with the goal of destroying Western culture and ruling as much territory as possible through fundamentalist Islam.

Chapter 3

Submission and Resistance

If you are so much under the control of the other person that you are fearful of doing anything other than what they want, then they have you where they want you.

—Dr. Raj Persaud, *Staying Sane*

Despite his mistakes, the Shah's rule was better for women than the Islamic state that followed. Women could work outside the home, albeit at wages much lower than their male counterparts. Women on television wore Western dress, used make-up, and sported stylish haircuts. Women drove cars and moved freely about the city. Iranian women had more freedom than in any other country in the Middle East.

Women had been Ayatollah Khomeini's biggest supporters, and without them, his return wouldn't have been possible. Khomeini never apologized for lying to them about the freedom they would have after the revolution. His plan had always been that women would have none.

After Khomeini took power, they watched in anger and shock as he stripped them of their rights. Iranian women had unleashed on themselves a brutal, backward dictatorship hiding behind the age-old cry of the oppressor: "I do this in the name of Islam, or national security, or fill-in-the-blank."

Women: The Underclass

In the new Islamic Republic of Iran, mullahs enacted sharia laws that ban women from being judges. Allegedly women have innate failings and lack ability, an idea borrowed from the sayings of Muhammad. The leaders of Iran are aware of how this looks to the rest of the world, so every now and then the Islamic Republic of Iran releases a long list of women judges, none of whom are actually judges.

Women inherit less than their male relatives; the testimony of a woman carries half the legal weight of a man's; a woman needs a father's or husband's permission for a passport and to leave the country; wives must have a husband's permission to work outside the home; a wife must have her husband's permission to get a higher education and go to college; and a woman can still be pressured to accept a polygamous marriage.

Women must ride at the back of the bus. They cluster there in their black chadors and hijabs—the epitome of inequality.

A man can travel, work and study where he pleases. Men make and interpret all of the laws. A wife must file for divorce, but a man can divorce her without her knowledge, and he can have multiple wives, including temporary wives or concubines.

Men still have to watch their step; an Islamic State doesn't want to pick up a male citizen's tab any more than any other country. But men can still dodge most of the bill. If a man divorces his wife, he has to pay a pre-agreed bridal gift. Some wives—out of humility, naiveté, or fear of force—ask only for a copy of the Quran. Sharia law is often interpreted to mean men pay only three months of alimony. At least some child support is required, but the ex-wife may have to battle in court to collect it.

Islamic Regimes: Legalized Pedophilia

The Prophet Muhammad practiced polygamy and had a total of around twelve wives, with possibly nine simultaneously. He owned and traded slaves and accepted the "gift" of a slave. Instead of freeing her, he made her a so-called wife. In his fifties, Muhammad "married" his friend's six-year-old daughter, Aisha, and took her into his house when she was nine.

Apologists say this was customary in the seventh century Middle East, but that doesn't make it right. Muhammad was a fierce critic of what he considered decadence in the Arab culture, yet he had sex with a nine-year-old child. Not only was the age gap between them more than forty years, but a young child is not capable of consent.

If Muhammad were alive today and living in the United States, he would be guilty of statutory rape. By U.S. standards, Islamic states that recognize marriages of nine-year-olds and other underage girls are enabling perverts.

Fundamentalist Islamic leaders both condone and legitimize pedophilia via marriage of children allowed by sharia laws; the supposed justification is that Muhammad himself married a prepubescent child. If Muslim leaders don't understand how repelled the West is by this stance, then they just aren't trying hard enough.

In the United States, we have strict laws against sex with children, as some former members of the Catholic priesthood and their enablers discovered. The United States prosecuted pedophile priests who preyed on both male and female victims. Catholics sued the Catholic Church and helped to imprison offending clergy. They recognize this for the abuse of power and trust that it is. Catholics find this behavior abhorrent and are trying to root it out.

In contrast, after Khomeini returned to Iran, he lowered the marriage age from sixteen to nine as long as the girl's father consented. After human rights activists drew international attention to it, the age was raised to a ridiculous thirteen. In 2013, Iran's parliament passed a law allowing men to marry their thirteen-year-old adopted daughters.[1] The Iranian Parliament is also trying to again roll back the marriage age to nine. With this kind of leadership, the Islamic Republic of Iran is a pedophile's paradise.

The Kingdom of Saudi Arabia is no better. In 2010, a nine-year-old Saudi girl was given away after her father quarreled with her mother. A twelve-year-old girl sued for divorce after she was forced to marry her father's eighty-year-old cousin.

Saudi Arabia is proposing a law so that women cannot be forced into marriage before the age of eighteen.[2] Why are they so slow to change? It is the only country in the world where women aren't allowed to drive, and women will first get the right to vote in 2015, unless 89-year-old King Abdullah changes his mind. His track record invites doubt.

King Abdullah has confined four of his adult daughters to dark quarters in his palace. The women have been prisoners for thirteen years. They are isolated and forbidden to see anyone. The women claim their uncles and half-brothers are complicit. In March 2014, Alanoud AlFayez, one of the King Abdullah's ex-wives, said her daughters are running out of food, and their only access to the outside world is the internet.[3] One of the daughters managed a telephone interview with *The New York Post*; she explained their crime was to fight for women's rights.[4]

Afghanistan is another haven for pedophiles. The fact-based film, *Osama*, is the story of a young girl living under the Taliban in Afghanistan. She disguises herself as a boy to go to school and uses the name Osama to avoid detection. When she begins menstruating, her deception is discovered, and she is harshly punished. Among other punishments, she is suspended in a well. A middle-aged mullah rescues her from further torture and possible execution, to add her to his collection of wives.

There is a Grand Canyon-sized difference between Islam and Catholicism. Pope Francis I, the head of the Catholic Church, has said that around 2% of Catholic priests are pedophiles, and child abuse is a scourge of the Church. The Pope added, "I find this state of affairs intolerable."[5]

Islamic Dress: Symbol of Death for Women's Rights

The warning signs flashed even before Khomeini returned. Clerics rolled back women's rights slowly at first. The Shahanshahi Club was a gathering place for well-off Iranians and well-heeled expatriates doing business in Iran. When I played tennis there, I wore the type of conservative white tennis dress that you might have seen at the time on center court at Wimbledon. When the Islamic fundamentalists gathered power, the dress code changed.

Men spied for the mullahs and watched women play. Stalkers for Islam. At first, tennis dresses were banned. We had to wear tennis shorts. A few weeks later, we were told to wear white slacks instead of shorts. Next we were told to wear long-sleeved shirts with the pants. Later, we were told to add a head scarf.

Shortly after Ayatollah Ruhollah Khomeini returned, the Shahanshahi Club was renamed the Revolutionary Club. Tennis was banned as the decadent capitalist game the deranged ayatollah believed it to be.

Khomeini immediately brought back the hijab, which required that women cover everything except their hands and face, act demurely, keep their eyes averted, and never challenge men. Both men and women were instantly confused, because Islamic dress codes are open to wide interpretation. Did the new rule mean cover all of your hair, or just most of it with a head scarf? If you guessed wrong and ran into the wrong mullah, you could be assaulted in the street.

Islamic clerics wanted women to wear the chador, and people in the souk, the marketplace and traditional news center, spread the word. When several uninformed women showed up at the souk without the chador, fanatics threw acid in their faces.

Women had no choice but to comply. Some wore the hijab, cloaked clothes with scarves to cover their hair. The religious or fearful wore a black chador. Women who showed too much hair risked a public beating, and those who fought back took the worst beatings.

Today Iran is licentious compared to Afghanistan. Nose jobs and hair dye are wildly popular, just as they were during the Shah's reign. Iranian women can smoke, drive, vote, and dress with a little more freedom. But not much more. Religious women still wear black chadors where only their face shows; others wear a knee-length manto and a head scarf, and mullahs push Iranian women to be more conservative.

In May 2007, hundreds of Iranian women were arrested on the streets, because they violated "correct" Islamic dress code: their hair peeked out from head scarves, or their hips weren't completely cloaked, or their jeans and heels could be seen.[6]

Policewomen in black chadors loaded women with "bad hijab" into buses that whisked them to police stations. The government plays women off each other. If the policewomen feed the "bad hijab girls" to the crocodiles, perhaps the crocodiles will be full by the time they get to them.

In October of 2014, four men threw acid on several women in Esfahan, Iran's third largest city. Nasser Jowrkesh told BBC Persian her daughter suffered acid burns on her face, hands, and legs. Acid blinded her right eye, and a surgeon held out little hope for saving any vision in her left eye.[7]

Iran's judiciary denies the attacks are linked to enforcing Islamic dress, but no one believes that spin. Ahmad Shouhani, an Iranian politician said, "Any improper veiling should be punished by law, not individually." He unhelpfully suggested the women somehow required punishment, as if evil thugs don't trust Iran's state-sanctioned victimization of women to do the job to their satisfaction.

The perpetrators were arrested and could face the death penalty, especially because the international media has reported the story; meanwhile, fundamentalists have been pushing a bill to protect vigilantes who enforce Islamic law.

Fundamentalist political group Ansar-e-Hezbollah, privately funded by conservatives, recently backed down from deploying 4,000 volunteers to flood the streets of Tehran and issue verbal warnings to women who aren't dressed in a manner hardliners see fit. But they will try again.[8]

Do people in the West object to veils? Not per se. Nuns often wear habits that cover their bodies and veil their hair. They made this choice as adults. Several orders of nuns have abandoned habits and dress in modest secular clothing customary for the time and place. Many are teachers and nurses in the most downtrodden countries in the world.

The West doesn't object to modest clothing, it objects to compulsory modest clothing. In many Islamic countries, women are compelled to adopt cumbersome clothing, and young girls are taught that they won't have a choice in the matter when their time comes. There's nothing morally superior about it. Mullahs have perverted this in such a way that the dress codes symbolize intolerance and abuse of women.

Fundamentalist Islamic dress codes range from a long coat and hair scarf called the *maghnaen* in Iran, to the niqab that covers everything except for the eyes, and the burqa in Afghanistan that covers everything and has a little screen through which women can barely see out.

Women obviously can't actively engage in outdoor sports in these clothes, so it's harder for them to stay fit. With so much of their bodies covered, women have little exposure to the sun and may not be absorbing enough vitamin D to metabolize calcium. If a woman developed rickets as a result, you wouldn't be able to tell with Islamic clothing.

You also wouldn't be able to tell if she has bruises or broken bones.

One day my neighbors' Filipino nanny frantically knocked on my door clutching their son in her arms. She was crying and clearly in distress.

"Come quick, lady," she pleaded, "something is happening."

I walked quickly to the next house and found my neighbor beating his wife. He had grown up in a well-to-do family, had been educated abroad, was wealthy in his own right, and wasn't a drunk. He used force as a means to control his wife, and he enjoyed it.

When he saw me, he gave me a sly crooked grin, and threw a dish at me. I ducked, and it missed. Now I was angry, and I shouted in English while moving forward. Maybe his wife felt she had to take it, but I didn't. He stopped this particular beating, probably because he didn't know what I'd do next. Neither did I, but whatever I decided, he wouldn't have liked it.

His wife later explained that her father was dead, and she had no brothers. When an Iranian man knows that a woman has no protectors and no money of her own, he can get away with whatever he wants to do.

Her mother encouraged her to divorce this brute, but she was afraid. Before her marriage, she agreed to a settlement in the event of divorce: a copy of the Quran, instead of money. She thought her husband would resist paying alimony and child support; furthermore, her mother had limited means. Theoretically, she could take her fight to court, but she was timid.

Domestic violence occurs in the United States, which is why we have shelters for battered women, restraining orders, and other means of trying to protect women. But I had never seen a man strike a woman until I lived in Iran.

Whatever the frequency, it does seem that Islamic states enable this kind of abuse by isolating women, clothing them restrictively, and depriving them of economic power.

What do Muslim women do when given a choice?

The first thing women in the Islamic Republic of Afghanistan did in 2001, when the Taliban was overthrown, was to shed the burqa, and they continue to fight for their rights.[9] By 2011, jihadists regained a foothold. They throw acid in women's faces and slice off breasts. Women wear the burqa to avoid getting attacked.[10] With the reduction in U.S. troops starting in 2014, and complete withdrawal by 2016, women's rights will probably roll back to the Stone Age.

Blame the Rape Victim's "Satanic Allure"

There is never a good reason for rape, but many Islamic leaders haven't gotten the memo. Fundamentalist Islam gives male rapists a ready and ridiculous excuse. If a woman is alone with a man she is asking for it, because men can't control themselves. It is obviously a woman's fault if she is raped, even if the "woman" is nine years old.

The body of a woman is considered to hold satanic allure. An unveiled woman is a source of decadence. She is dangerous to a young man. Women must defer to men, and domestic violence against women isn't prosecuted.

Those are the misogynistic lessons taught in the world of fundamentalist Islam.

Rape is a tragedy in any circumstance, but it is life-threatening for survivors in fundamentalist regimes. It is no surprise that women don't want to report it. Muslim women who have been raped have dishonored their families and are treated as outcasts or beaten to death in "honor killings." The culture that existed in this region was already backward before Muhammad and Islam arrived on the scene. Islam simply codified the backwardness. The tragedy is that this repression did not have to happen. Well before Islam, there were enlightened men.

St. Augustine, Bishop of Hippo, was one of the most influential philosophers in the Catholic Church. Seven years after the 410 A.D. sack of Rome, he wrote *The City of God* and gave his views on rape:

> An attack on one's body may inflict not merely physical pain, but may also excite carnal pleasure...I affirm, therefore, that in case of violent rape and of an unshaken intention not to yield unchaste

> consent, the crime is attributable only to the ravisher and not at all to the ravished. [11]

St. Augustine also maintained that no woman lost her chastity because of a violation. His is a very different narrative than you hear from fundamentalist Islamic leaders, and I believe that St. Augustine's philosophy is the enlightened one.

This isn't to say the Catholic Church as a whole is enlightened. Some of the thirteenth century writings of St. Thomas Aquinas are blatantly misogynistic. Ireland's government colluded with Catholics to enslave and abuse thousands of women and girls in Magdalene Laundries run by nuns, criminals actually, as recently as the 1980s.[12] Modest clothing, whatever the religion, doesn't necessarily imply goodness. Every religion has its fundamentalists and fanatics.

India is 80% Hindu and only around 13% Muslim. Hindu women decry "India's rape culture" and its culture of impunity for Hindu rapists.[13]

A few decades ago, it was common for male judges in U.S. courts to blame rape victims for their dress or demeanor, and that attitude made prosecutions difficult.

Even the U.S. military has its problems. On March 10, 1994, *The New York Times* reported on abuse heaped on military women who reported sexual harassment. Lieutenant Darlene Simmons, a lawyer in the Navy Reserve, was forced to take a psychiatric exam after she accused her commander of harassment in 1991 and 1992. Before the accusation Lieutenant Simmons said she had a spotless record as a successful attorney; after her complaint, she was branded a troublemaker, and her career in the Navy was ruined.

Sergeant Zenaida Martinez, a military police officer in the Air Force, said this about her superior's advances in 1992: "He explicitly described the benefits of my having a sexual relationship with him...made me understand that if I refused, my career would suffer."[14]

She refused. She said her car's tires were slashed, and unbeknownst to her, documents alleging negative performance and misconduct were placed in her personnel file. She became the focus of the official enquiry, not the man. She said the Air Force legal system treated the complaining victim—not the perpetrator—as a threat to the organization.

More than twenty years later, Senator Kirsten Gillibrand is fighting the military hierarchy to change its ways. She explains that victims—more than half of the U.S. military's rape victims are men—do not trust their chain of command, and with good reason.

In her 2014 book, *Off the Sidelines*, Senator Gillibrand writes that Major General Vaughn Ary defended the system of keeping all legal decisions in the chain of command, asserting it was necessary to maintain "good order and discipline." Gillibrand retorted: "By what accounting were nineteen thousand sexual assaults a year good order and discipline?"[15]

The military is a unique and unbalanced system in the United States. Its rigid hierarchy resists change. But Senator Gillibrand and other members of Congress got rid of "Don't ask, don't tell," allowing gays to serve openly in the military, and they are working on an objective third-party review system for rape cases.

The fact that many victims are men illustrates what happens when any underclass has little recourse, and the underclass's testimony doesn't carry full weight: the underclass is ripe for victimization. To reverse this, objective third party oversight is essential.

If Islamic clerics, who control the court system and make the laws, wish to claim that men can't help themselves, and women are a source of temptation, then no reasonable man or woman should trust that hierarchy for justice.

In fact, there's no recourse at all in many countries where terrorists hide behind fundamentalist Islam. In May 2014, First Lady Michelle Obama condemned the April kidnapping of nearly 300 schoolgirls by Nigerian al-Qaeda-linked terrorist group Boko Haram.[16] The group's name roughly translates as "non-Islamic education is forbidden." The group's leader threatened to sell the girls into slavery. In

September, one of the girls was found "heavily traumatized" in the forest, and none of the girls has been rescued.[17]

Afghan President Hamid Karzai claims to be a supporter of women's rights, yet Afghanistan is one of the worst places in the world to be female. In Afghanistan, if rape victims file a report, they are prosecuted for "moral crimes." In March 2014, Franz-Michael Skyjold Mellbin, the new EU Ambassador to Kabul, expressed outrage:

> [The prosecution of] moral crimes is something that is a scourge for women in Afghanistan, it means that girls and women who are victims ... are further victimised by the state. It's a disgrace for any country to have such an institution.[18]

Yet the West, with a growing population of Islamic immigrants, has bent over backwards in a misguided attempt to be politically correct. Our free speech suffers for it; women's rights suffer for it; and our free society suffers for it.

"Appalling Depravity" and Political Expediency

In an October 1, 2001, commentary for *The Independent,* Yasmin Alibhai-Brown decried Pakistan's suppression of seventy incest cases, punishment of rape victims, honor murders, and other violent violations of women's rights:

> I don't want anyone else to enlighten me about what the Koran [alternate spelling of Quran] says on women; what I would like is a robust dialogue about what we can do to stop the cruelties against women and girls in the Muslim world. This oppression is not confined to Muslim countries, of course. But we have an obligation to clean up our own backyards and to tell and confront the complicated truth.[19]

I would like to add that the unvarnished truth is easier to tell when you are no longer living in a country ruled by Islamic leadership, but that isn't always true.

In England, the Rotherham Metropolitan Borough Council published an independent inquiry into the rapes and gang rapes from 1997-2003 of around 1,400 mainly white or mixed race girls by men mainly from the Muslim Pakistani community in the town. Some of the men were old enough to be the girls' grandfathers, and some of the girls, including many children, were traded as sex slaves. In many cases, social care blamed the exploited children characterizing them as "out of control." According to the report:

> We read cases where a child was doused in petrol and threatened with being set alight, children who were threatened with guns, children who witnessed brutally violent rapes and were threatened that they would be the next victim if they told anyone. Girls as young as 11 were raped by large numbers of male perpetrators, one after the other.[20]

When Sue Reid reported victims' accounts for the *Daily Mail,* detractors tried to destroy her reputation. She was completely vindicated by the evidence and summed it up in her August 26, 2014 article titled, "I was called a liar and a racist for exposing this sex gang abuse horror."[21]

Who were the actual racists? The Pakistani gangs referred to the victims, mostly from poor backgrounds, as "white trash."

Reid quoted a confidential police report leaked to British newspapers: "There is a problem with networks of Muslim offenders both locally and nationally." Reid also reported that when Mohammed Shafiq, director of a Muslim charitable organization, spoke up and gave early warning about the abuse of girls, he became the target of death threats.

The perpetrators seemed to be equal opportunity predators. Pakistani women were also exploited. The UK Muslim Women's Network's September 2013 report highlighted thirty-five case studies of mostly Muslim girls across the UK, victimized by mostly Muslim men. The abuse was similar to that reported in Rotherham. Girls feared they would be ostracized by their own communities if they reported the abuse.

Authorities turned a blind eye and ignored or suppressed credible reports of "appalling depravity" for years. According to Home Secretary Teresa May, it was a "complete dereliction of duty" by the town's council for reasons of political expediency.

Labor MP Denis MacShane—jailed for filing phony expense claims—said he avoided investigating the sexual abuse by gangs of criminals in the Muslim community, because of "misplaced racial sensitivity," and he didn't want to "rock the multi-cultural boat."[22,23]

If all it takes is for criminals to use the word "racism" to commit horrific acts and get away with them, then Rotherham needs a complete overhaul of its government.

Under the Dome

Iran's Islamic Republic wrote the script for brainwashing women, and many Islamic countries have a variation on this theme.

Brainwashers are emotional abusers, and their effect is to make women feel powerless and dependent.

They use the following techniques: 1) control of finances by limiting a woman's ability to get an income-producing job and inherit wealth, 2) control of the physical environment, including where she can travel, 3) not discussing plans, such as the ability of a man to divorce a woman without her knowledge, 4) forcing new behaviors and attitudes on women, such as making women wear restrictive clothing, and 5) what the brainwasher says is the final word. For example, when Khomeini was alive, he claimed he was infallible and his interpretation of sharia law was the only correct one.

In his book, *Learned Optimism*, psychologist Martin E.P. Seligman, Ph.D. explains that people who feel helpless show psychomotor retardation and diminished energy:

> People given unsolvable problems reported that a depressed mood descended on them. They didn't fight back when attacked or insulted.[24]

Women with some spirit left will look for a way out. Unfortunately, in Islamic countries, they have few options.

Refusing to Submit

On February 21, 1994, women's rights activist Dr. Homa Darabi walked into a square in Iran, doused herself with gasoline, and set herself ablaze. She died of her self-inflicted injuries.

Under the Shah's rule, SAVAK had arrested then released her. She and her husband decamped to the United States where she practiced psychiatry. Darabi was the first Iranian to be accepted to the American Board of Psychiatry and Neurology. When the Shah was overthrown, Dr. Darabi returned to her homeland to help, but her help was unwanted in the Islamic Republic. Officials took away her right to practice medicine. Her final fiery protest was her response.

*****

Shirin Ebadi became Iran's first female judge under the Shah's regime. After the revolution, women could no longer be judges, but by the 1990s Ms. Ebadi was able to practice as a lawyer.

Ebadi lobbied to increase the age of child marriage from nine to thirteen in Iran and pushed for the concession that women could raise their male children until the boys were seven years old, a right the Islamic Republic of

Iran had taken from them. Compared to freedoms women had under the Shah's regime, these are small concessions, but it doesn't appear they will stick. The age at which girls can be forced into "marriage" will probably be rolled back to nine.

In 2003, Ebadi became the first Iranian to win the Nobel Peace Prize; it should have been the Appeasement Prize. She was tolerated, because she wasn't a strong activist. Her changes were incremental, and at times she went along to get along.[25]

In a January 2004 *Frontline* interview, Ebadi claimed Islam is not a religion of terror and violence; there is no "clash of civilizations."[26] Who was she trying to kid? The religious leaders in Iran use death fatwas and terrorist tactics to suppress protests, and sharia law clashes with Western civilization. It is no wonder the Iranian government allowed her to be the figurehead for women's rights for so long; she disseminated soothing propaganda.

In June 2003, around 4,000 Iranian university students were arrested after protesting for reform. Many were thrown into solitary confinement, some were given long prison sentences, and others were killed. Families of protesters who were shot had to pay for the bullets used to kill their children and were denied a burial ceremony. Other students simply disappeared.

Iranian-Canadian journalist Zahra Kazemi photographed a bloody dormitory scene where dozens of students were murdered. She was arrested.

Her captors made her stand while they insulted and pushed her. Iranian prisoners know they are supposed to take abuse without standing up to their oppressors. Kazemi, however, refused to submit. Her defiance enraged them. Officials spent the next seventy-seven hours beating, raping, and torturing her to death.[27,28]

Zahra Kazemi was murdered on July 11, 2003, three months before Shirin Ebadi accepted her Nobel Peace Prize, and just six months before Ebadi's *Frontline* interview. In subsequent court proceedings, Ebadi represented the late Kazemi's side, but Mohammad Reza Aghdam Ahmadi, a low-level scapegoat, was acquitted.

In 2009, Shirin Ebadi moved to the UK to escape incessant persecution. After she fled, she finally admitted that the Iranian sharia-based judiciary system is "a subsidiary of the Intelligence Ministry."[29]

Female Genital Mutilation (FGM)

Female genital mutilation is practiced in various forms of severity in at least twenty-eight Muslim countries. This practice predates Islam, and it isn't practiced in every Muslim country. For example, to the best of my knowledge, it is not, and never has been, a custom in Iran. Saudi Arabia condemns the practice. Where it is practiced, it is enabled by local Muslim clergy—instead of being denounced by them—and locals believe it is a religious requirement.[30]

There are no health benefits for women, but there are grave health risks, including infection, excessive bleeding, urinary problems, and more. Yet, some mullahs claim Muhammad allowed it, so it cannot be forbidden.

Muslim males are circumcised, as are Jewish males and more than 50% of males in the United States (in the U.S. it is done for health and hygiene). The Quran does not mention circumcision, at least based on my reading of an English translation. In Islam, male circumcision is a religious custom—not a law set out in the Quran—and is known as sunnah, a tradition consistent with the hadiths, the practices and teachings of Muhammad. But for females, submission to this violent life-altering act is called an "honorable deed" by those who seek to defend the indefensible.

Female genital mutilation immigrated to the United States with fundamentalist Muslims from countries with this custom.[31] A report by New York based Sanctuary for Families, "Female Genital Mutilation in the United States," cites a 1997 report from the Centers for Disease Control and Prevention that estimated at least 150,000 to 200,000 Muslim girls were at risk of mutilation. This practice is, of course, banned in the United States, so there are no actual records of how often it occurs.

Sanctuary for Families asserts that due to immigration from the twenty-eight African and Middle Eastern countries that practice FGM, even more U.S. based females—more than 200,000 girls—are at risk today.[32]

Girls are sometimes sent away for "vacation" cutting to countries that practice FGM. Sometimes it is done in the U.S. In this shadowy world, untrained women often use razor blades or crude instruments, and they do not administer anesthetic.

The U.S. hasn't passed laws to prevent this. In France, there have been at least 100 successful prosecutions and prison sentences for parents who allowed their daughters to be mutilated. In the U.S. there has only been one. In 2006, an Ethiopian immigrant was sentenced to ten years in prison after he removed his two-year-old daughter's clitoris with a scissors.[33]

Theoretically, Islamic law protects a woman's right to sexual enjoyment, and, theoretically, a woman can divorce her husband if he does not provide her with sexual satisfaction. At least that's one interpretation.

The current reality is that women's sexual rights aren't protected. Some followers of Islam are determined to control female sexuality to the point that a woman's satisfaction is not merely irrelevant, it is destroyed.

Ayaan Hirsi Ali was born a Muslim in Somalia and spent the first eight years of her life there before moving to Saudi Arabia, Ethiopia, Kenya, Denmark, and, finally, the United States. Somalia is a tragic place to be born a female. One in 100 women die in childbirth; only the South Sudan and Chad have worse maternal death rates. One in ten babies are born dead; only Afghanistan and Mali have worse infant mortality rates. If that weren't bad enough, in Somalia, Muslims practice female genital mutilation.

Western media calls female genital mutilation female "circumcision," but the cuts in Somalia are not circum anything; they go right to the core. The mutilation includes an excision of the critical nerves that give women sexual pleasure. If anything is left behind that can stimulate a woman's response, it is purely accidental and due to lack of sufficient education in mutilation. It is as if the fundamentalist Muslims who practice FGM fear female orgasms.

Forced mutilation is an attempt to create female eunuchs with no desire to initiate sex, only to be available when men want intercourse. Virgin brides are prized. The goal is ultimate control of female sexuality and the destruction of the essence of a strong feminine personality.

In a March 14, 2013, interview with Alison Roberts of the *London Evening Standard*, Ayaan Hirsi Ali offers valuable insight as to why this problem hasn't been eradicated:

> It was done to me at the age of five, and 10 years later, even 20 years later, I would not have testified against my parents. It is a psychological issue. The people who are doing this are fathers, mothers, grandmothers, aunts. No little girl is going to send them to prison. How do you live with that guilt?[34]

In her teens in Kenya, Hirsi Ali had a Saudi-funded Muslim education and sympathized with the Muslim Brotherhood, unusual in Kenya. Upon further study, she rejected those views and now is an outspoken critic of Islam. With director Theo van Gogh, she made a 2004 English short film, *Submission*, a fictional story of Muslim women who experienced abuse. Within the film, an actress wears a partially transparent chador and quotes verses of the Quran.

In November 2004, Mohammed Bouyeri, a Dutch Muslim, assassinated Theo van Gogh. *The Independent* reported van Gogh's last words:

> He shot Van Gogh twice in the chest. Van Gogh howled: "Can't we talk about this?" Bouyeri ignored his pleas and fired four more times. Then he pulled out a knife and slit Van Gogh's throat with

> such strength that his head was almost severed from his body. He used the other knife to stab a five-page letter [addressed to Hirsi Ali] onto Van Gogh's hemorrhaging corpse.[35]

Ayaan Hirsi Ali is now a U.S. citizen and the author of several books on her life experiences with Islam. She expressed a controversial view to Roger van Bakel during an interview in *Reason*: Islam will only bring about change if it is "defeated" so that the peace-seeking Muslims, who she says are passive and not following the rules of Islam, can prevail. She expanded, "I think that we are at war with Islam. And there's no middle ground in wars....you stop the spread of the ideology itself."[36] In a 2007 *New York Times* interview, she called fundamentalist Islam "a destructive, nihilistic cult of death."[37]

According to Ayaan Hirsi Ali, in the eyes of a fundamentalist, there is no such thing as a moderate Muslim. Fundamentalist Muslims call her an "Islamophobe." They object to her ideas, which are about objectionable ideas within the teachings of Islam today.

Unveiled Threat

Malala Yousafzai became the youngest person to win the Nobel Peace Prize after she used a pseudonym to write a BBC blog for three years on repression under Taliban rule in Pakistan's Swat valley.[37] The fundamentalists closed schools and banned education for girls. When her blogging identity became known, she was awarded Pakistan's National Youth Peace Prize and became recognizable. Death threats followed.

As she rode the school bus home on October 9, 2012, the Taliban stopped the vehicle and demanded to know which of them was Malala. Several of her classmates looked in her direction; Malala's was the only uncovered face. The Taliban opened fire. Two bullets missed, but one hit her in the head, and she underwent numerous surgeries in Pakistan and England. She refused to be silenced. In another act of courageous defiance, she wrote about the ordeal in her book, *I am Malala*, and uses her global prominence to lobby for women's education.[38]

Fundamentalists use a disingenuous bullhorn, physical intimidation, monetary pressure, and violence to impose their ideology on others. In the world of fundamentalist Islam, an independent-minded woman who refuses to submit is an unveiled threat.

Chapter 4

The Religion of Intolerance

Perhaps for these fifty years past no one has ever heard a dogmatical expression escape me.

—Benjamin Franklin

The CIA World Factbook counts the world's population at more than 7 billion people, and approximately 1.6 billion are Muslims. Only around 15%, or 240 million Muslims, are Arabs. Indonesia's population of 253 million includes around 222 million Muslims. The Republic of India has a population of 1.2 billion, of which 15% or 166 million are Muslims. If you combine Indian Muslims with the 189 million Muslims in Pakistan, they add up to around 355 million, 115 million more than the number of Arab Muslims.

Muslims are in the majority in around forty-nine countries, but Muslims are the minority in most Western countries. They make up less than

1% of the U.S. population. Most United States citizens, around 77%, are Christian. France is 5-10% Muslim, but Muslims make up fewer than 5% of the populations of Canada, Germany, the United Kingdom, Denmark, and the Netherlands.

The Quran, Five Pillars, and Literature of Sihah Hadiths (Sunnah)

According to Philip Hitti's *The Arabs,* when Muhammad ibn Abdullah was born in 570 AD, Mecca had hundreds of shrines to different gods, and chaotic violence kept society in an uproar. Muhammad, a well-traveled businessman, observed Christians and Jews; he came to appreciate the unifying power of monotheism and having one sacred book. He chose one of the ancient gods of Mecca, a deity people invoked in times of great danger, and declared, "There is no God but Allah!"[1] Islam means submission to the will of Allah.

Disaffected young men rallied to Muhammad's cry. Muhammad led a violent band who murdered, raped, and traded slaves. It was part of their program to gain converts. Islam will only be a religion of peace after it has conquered all non-believers, but since no one knows how Muslim is Muslim enough for a fundamentalist, there is no telling when Islamic-based conflicts will end.

Muhammad and his followers founded a society based on Islamic rule in 622 AD, which marks the first year of the Muslim calendar. The basis for Islamic rule is the Quran, which Muslims believe is the verbatim record of Allah's words, as revealed to Muhammad by the Angel Gabriel, and they are to follow these exact words, without alteration, for all time. Every day, Muslims hear the call to prayer sung out from minarets of mosques. The entire Islamic world says their prayers in Arabic, and for fundamentalists there will never be a Quran 2.0.

Fundamentalists consider the Five Pillars of Islam to be mandatory for all believers: 1) Profession of faith or *shahada*: "There is no God but Allah, and Muhammad is the messenger of Allah"; 2) Prayer, in Arabic, five times a day: dawn, noon, mid-afternoon, sunset and dusk; 3) Alms-giving; 4) Fasting from dawn to sunset during the month of Ramadan, the time when the Angel Gabriel gave the Quran to Muhammad; and 5) The hajj, or pilgrimage to Mecca in Saudi Arabia, at least once in a lifetime. An estimated 15 million people visit Mecca each year, and of those, around 3 million do the formal pilgrimage.

The Quran contains Allah's words, but nothing of Muhammad's biography. Muslims acknowledge a collection of literature called Sahih hadiths, or Sunnah—records of Muhammad's teachings—as reliable histories of the deeds and sayings of Muhammad. They believe he is the Perfect Man, someone to emulate.

Technically, Muslims who do not follow the Quran are not following the rules of Islam and are not genuine Muslims, any more than a Catholic who does not accept the pope as the leader of the Church is a genuine Catholic.

I do not quote passages of the Quran or of the hadiths in this book. Instead, I focus on the behavior of those who say they follow these teachings. Apologists claim that offensive passages are taken out of context or that a word in Arabic doesn't mean what the English translator thought it meant. That excuse doesn't work anymore. Multiple English translations are widely available; some are even free electronic downloads. Most of the Muslim world doesn't speak Arabic or English as their mother tongue. Are all of their translations incorrect?

Arab countries are funding terrorists who commit crimes in the name of Islam. That isn't coming out of nowhere; it is directly tied to their interpretation of fundamentalist Islam as written in the original Arabic.

Moderate Muslims claim they take the parts of the Quran and hadiths that are consistent with life in the 21st century and promote peaceful coexistence. They've adopted Quran 2.0—even though they may never have fully read the original Quran—and they have formed a new religion: Moderate Islam. Yet, moderates haven't acknowledged a schism, the birth of a heretical new religion, and they still call themselves Muslims. Fundamentalist Muslims consider these updates by moderate Muslims to be a pernicious virus.

Beheadings Don't Open Minds

In September 2014, His Excellency Iyad Ameen Madani, Secretary General of the Organization of Islamic Cooperation, told an assembly of the Chicago Council on Global Affairs that people should not make fun of Muhammad, because it hurts the feelings of Muslims. The Secretary General made a fair, but incomplete, point.

It is important to keep an open mind, but not so open that your brains fall out. Certainly we can all agree that good manners are valued everywhere, and rudeness is something to be avoided. But many Muslim clerics and their followers go very far out of their way to take offense; then give offense out of proportion to the stimulus.

Pakistani cleric Mohammed Yousaf Qureshi issued a death fatwa in 2006 and offered a $1 million bounty after a Danish cartoonist drew caricatures of the prophet Muhammad: "Whoever insults the prophet deserves to be killed and whoever will take this insulting man to his end will get this prize."[2]

Qureshi not only wants to infringe on one's right to free speech, he has crossed the line into inciting terrorism. Qureshi cannot hide behind the word "religion" to justify this. He is a criminal, and he is not alone.

Fundamentalist Muslims engaged in violent protests in Pakistan and India. In Peshawar, effigies of Danish, German, French, and Norwegian leaders were hung from lampposts. In the Punjab, rioters defiled the Danish flag and chanted: "We are slaves of the prophet."

One man's joke may be another man's insult, but there are limits in a civilized society to what we can do when we believe someone else has been rude. Moreover, there is a matter of free speech. Every quip or joke cannot be characterized as hate speech or an insult to the prophet punishable with violence.

Gays Are Persecuted

When it comes to insults, it seems the gay community in fundamentalist Islamic countries is very familiar with them. Arsham Parsi, founder of the Persian Gay and Lesbian Organization, fled Iran after three of his friends committed suicide, and after authorities started following him and arrested another two of his friends. His two sisters were expelled from university because of his advocacy of gay rights.[3]

It is astonishing that Iran provides financial assistance for transgender surgeries and is second only to Thailand for the number of operations, until you learn that, according to Parsi, nearly half of the operations are performed on gays (who are not transgender).[4]

The Gulf Cooperation Council of Bahrain, Kuwait, Saudi Arabia, UAE, Qatar, and Oman ban homosexuality. Homosexuals are persecuted in Yemen, Iraq, and fourteen African countries.[5]

In July 2014, Saudi Arabia sentenced a gay man to three years and 450 lashes, to be meted out in fifteen sessions of thirty lashes each, for using Twitter to communicate with other homosexuals.[6,7]

Saudi Arabia: Only Mosques Allowed

Saudi Arabia's flag is green, the color of Islam. The profession of faith is written in Arabic calligraphy underscored by a sword, the ideology of fundamentalist Islam.

The genesis of power for the Saudi royal family was fundamentalist ideology that united previously warring tribes. The Saudis adopted the conservative Sunni teachings of Muhammad ibn Abd al-Wahhab, a mid-1700s Muslim reformer. They returned to the pure faith with its social consequences: subjugation of women, cutting off hands for thievery, stoning to punish adultery, and beheadings for various violations. The alliance of mutual promotion was successful, and by 1932, the tiny Saudi state grew to become the Kingdom of Saudi Arabia.

Most of the Muslim world calls Saudis Wahhabis, but most Saudis prefer the word *Muwahhidun* (monotheist) or simply Muslim, because they believe their interpretation of fundamentalist Islam is the only genuine one. Of the 27 million Saudis, there are around 4 million Salafis; they don't like to be called Wahhabis, because Salafis are even more fundamentalist.

Saudi Arabia tries to portray itself as moderate. Grand Mufti Abdul Aziz Al-Asheikh, the top religious leader in Saudi Arabia, gave a speech in Mecca at the 2004 hajj and reminded the pilgrims that Islam does not countenance hijacking planes and terrorism—at least when it comes to other Sunni Muslims.

Yet in Saudi Arabia, only mosques are allowed. The practice of any religion other than Islam must be done in private. One may not eat, drink even water, or smoke in public during Ramadan, and the law is strictly enforced whether or not one is Muslim.

In 2012, the Saudi Grand Mufti Abdul Aziz Al-Asheikh, who is also head of the Permanent Committee for Islamic Research and Issuing Fatwas, discredited any pretense of religious tolerance when he issued a fatwa calling for the destruction of all the churches on the Arabian Peninsula.[8]

On September 17, 2001, then-President George Bush claimed "Islam is Peace."[9] On September 24, 2014, President Obama gave a speech to the United Nations General Assembly asking them to confront extremists and said, "Islam teaches peace."[10] But Grand Mufti Abdul Aziz Al-Asheikh's fatwa suggests Islam is the religion of "smash churches of other faiths to pieces."

Middle East: Countries, Ethnicity, and Religion

The Arab League was founded on March 22, 1945. Its headquarters is in Cairo, Egypt. The league has 22 member countries: Algeria, Bahrain, Comoro Islands, Djibouti, Egypt, Iraq, Jordan, Kuwait, Lebanon, Libya, Mauritania, Morocco, Oman, Palestine, Qatar, Saudi Arabia, Somalia, Sudan, Syria, Tunisia, United Arab Emirates, and Yemen. Iranians, Indonesians, South American, North American, Chinese and other non-Arab Muslims obviously are not included.

The league's primary objective is to unite Arab countries in politics, economics, and country infrastructure. Since Islam is interwoven with the politics of these countries, it is automatically part of the league's unification objective. Arabs are mostly Sunni Muslims.

The Arab homeland covers 5.25 million square miles, about 145% of the area of the United States. It spans the region from the Atlantic coast of northern Africa in the west to the Arabian Sea in the east, and from the Mediterranean Sea in the north to Central Africa in the south. Only about 60% of the people living in the Arab homeland speak Arabic.

Iran is not part of the Arab homeland. Around 90% of Iranians are Shiite Muslims, and most Iranians are Aryans. Most Iranians do not speak Arabic, even though Iran uses Arabic script for writing, the way French and English use the same script but are different languages. The official language of Iran is Farsi, an Indo-European language.

The Middle East is riddled with multiple languages, dialects, unique cultures, ethnic groups, and religious factions that often overlap.

Ethnic groups include Arabs, Aryans, Kurds, Turks, Persians, Azeris, Luris, Balochis, Assyrians, Punjabis, Pashtuns, Afro-Asians and more.

Muslim sects include Sunnis, Wahhabis, Shias, Salafis, Sufis, Ismaelis, Ahmedis, Alawites, and Seveners. Christians, Jews, and ancient religions are also at home in the Middle East.

All of this is combined in clusters and separated by geographic lines, often arbitrarily drawn by Europeans who were foreign to the region. This is confusing both to foreigners and to those born in the Middle East.

Sunnis versus Shias: Arabs and Aryans

The two main Muslim sects are Sunni and Shia, but according to a 2009 Pew Research report, Shias are only about 10-15% of the Muslim population, and Sunnis make up most of the rest.[11]

Muhammad died without a surviving male heir. Muslims quarreled bitterly over succession, and this dispute created two main factions: Sunnis and Shias. The result was a reign of terror.

Jihad originally referred to man's inner struggle to resist evil, but thanks to perpetual Islamic violence, in the West, jihad is synonymous with holy war. Sunnis and Shias battle to this day.

Sunnis recognize Abu Bakr, the father of Aisha who was "married" to Muhammad at the age of six, as the first caliph and Muhammad's successor; Shias recognize Ali, Muhammad's son-in-law, as the successor and call him "the first imam." Ali, Muhammad's first cousin, married Muhammad's daughter, Fatimah. The union produced two sons, Hasan and Husayn (often written as Hussein).

Ali was assassinated while praying at a mosque in Kufa in 661 AD. When Ali died, his sons became the successors in the eyes of the Shias, but the Sunnis already recognized another caliph, Muawia.

Ali's oldest son, Hasan, the Shias' second imam, took a large pension—a payoff—from Muawia and moved to Medina. Shias believe Muawia poisoned Hasan, so that Muawia's son Yazid would be his uncontested successor.

When Muawia died, Ali's younger son, Husayn, the Shias' third imam, refused to swear allegiance to Yazid and actively opposed him.

Yazid raised troops of assassins and encircled Husayn and seventy-one of his followers in the Karbala desert. Yazid's men denied them water, and in 680 AD, on the 10th day of Ramadan (Ashura), Yazid's men massacred all but a handful of Husayn's company.

According to Shias, the warriors desecrated Husayn's body, even though Husayn was Muhammad's grandson. Then they uncovered Husayn's sister Zaynab, Muhammad's granddaughter, and marched her all the way back to Damascus.

The first twelve imams were lousy military strategists; they were all assassinated. The Shias glorify this as martyrdom or *shahadat*, and mourn these events during Ashura. It is the Shias' biggest religious holiday. Shia Muslims revere imams both as leaders and saints who shine with an inner divine light. That's why Khomeini coveted the title, and that's why today's Shia leaders vie to be called imam.

Many Iranian male Shias, including my ex-husband, use the honorific prefix Sayed. This means they are patrilineal descendants of Muhammad's Arab grandsons Hasan and Husayn. They are not patrilineal descendants of Muhammad, but they are nonetheless Muhammad's descendants through his daughter Fatimah. Yet at the same time, most Iranians vehemently deny Arab heritage. They joke that 80% of Iranians have Arab blood, but only 2% will admit it. Only genetic testing will determine whether they are putting on religious airs or denying partial Arab ancestry.

Sunnis and Shias fight over succession, but there are differences among Shias, too. Take Iraq and Iran, for example. Around 60-65% of Iraq's 32 million people are Shias, and the rest are mostly Sunnis. Unlike Iranians, most Iraqi Shias are Arabs and speak Arabic.

After Khomeini's death in 1989, Iran's Ayatollah Ali Khameini claimed the title of imam. Meanwhile, in Iraq, Iranian-born Ayatollah Ali Sistani, a 73-year-old Shia, declared himself supreme leader. *The Wall Street Journal* quoted an Iraqi cleric: "Ayatollah Sistani has the last word. He is above any president, and his words are above the law."

In other words, Iraqi Shias and Iranian Shias recognize different religious leaders, speak different languages, and consider themselves to be different ethnic groups. So even among Shias there are conflicts.

Iran: Religious Persecution, Murder and Theft

Under the Shah's rule the small minority of Bahais, Christians, Hindus, Zoroastrians, and Jews freely practiced their religions and thrived. Yet there were signs of resentment.

An English-speaking mullah once asked me to sum up the Bible in one sentence. That's like asking Scheherazade to tell you a story.

Fortunately, there's a sentence I have always liked: "The Bible is the good news that God loves you."

For some reason my response angered him. He glared at me as if to say, *Infidel, Allah doesn't love you!* When I asked him for his one-sentence summary of the Quran, he launched into a diatribe about his imagined superiority of Islam.

My ex-husband and his entire family were secular Muslims. They never prayed. My husband didn't own a prayer rug, and he didn't own a copy of the Quran. I was a non-practicing Catholic. They were apostates, and I was an infidel. The number of times we discussed religious philosophy was exactly zero, but we discussed the symptoms of religious intolerance that manifested itself when Khomeini's supporters began to agitate for his return.

I saw how so-called moderate Muslims passively handed over an entire country to fundamentalists—as if they secretly harbored guilt for being bad Muslims. It was as if the supremacy of the fundamentalists emboldened many passive Muslims to embrace fundamentalism again. Resisters became a shrinking minority.

Christian Armenians owned a cluster of shops a few miles from where we lived. Their Iranian family lines went back for centuries. Even so, their businesses were targeted in a Nazi-style *Kristallnacht.* Muslim thugs smashed Armenian shop windows, looted stores, and warned Armenians to leave the country. Christians were no longer wanted.

After the Shah fled Iran, my husband and I attended a party, and a couple announced they were moving to Canada. They were fleeing because her grandfather was Jewish. My husband agreed it was a good idea to run.

Most Jews wouldn't have considered her Jewish, since neither her grandmother nor her mother were Jewish, but Iran's persecution was brutal and unpredictable. Why take a chance? They left early and were lucky.

After Khomeini returned, he perversely compelled non-Muslim religious leaders to sign statements that they had the right to freely practice their religions in Iran. But the official policy afterwards included wholesale persecution mixed with murder.

Habib Elghanian was a leader in Iran's thriving Jewish community, and his factories created jobs in Iran. His industriousness made him one of Iran's richest men, and he was a well-known philanthropist. My father-in-law imported foreign appliances, and Elghanian sometimes visited his shops to compare products. I had met him briefly at the Shahanshahi Club. He was a very pleasant man.

In May of 1979, Elghanian was tried on false charges, including an allegation of being a Zionist spy. He was given a brief, brutal televised trial and then executed immediately afterwards. Mullahs confiscated his property in the name of the Islamic revolution, which meant they would have a lifestyle upgrade.

I recalled Habib Elghanian's smile. His passing was the loss of a great contributor to Iran and a tremendous blow to the Jewish community. A shining light in the darkness of the Islamic Republic of Iran had been extinguished.

Albert Danielpour was executed in Hamadan, after he was accused of spying for Israel. Khomeini told Danielpour he wouldn't be killed, but another ayatollah gave him a quick night trial. Danielpour denied all the charges, and was murdered anyway. A dozen other Jews met the same fate.

Tens of thousands of Jews fled Iran. Many Jews who remained were denied business licenses, and their property was confiscated.

After a skiing accident, I saw a German-trained orthopedic specialist and began physical therapy at his offices. One day I showed up for therapy, and he wasn't there. His receptionist said no one seemed to be in his house, and no one could locate him. Then she burst into tears. She explained he was a Bahai, part of a religious sect Khomeini's followers denounced as heretics of Islam. We could only hope he had fled the country.

The Islamic revolution systematically persecuted Bahais and viewed them as heretics. Throughout the country, fundamentalist Muslims destroyed beautiful Bahai temples, and burned their homes.

In May of 2014, *Bahai World News Service* reported that Iran's Revolutionary Guards desecrated Bahai graves, including the graves of ten Bahai women lynched thirty years ago for teaching Sunday school.[12]

Zoroastrianism, founded in Persia in the sixth century B.C., was tolerated under the Shah. Its chief deity, Ahura Mazda, stands for light and wisdom. Khomeini viewed it as paganism.

Sunni Muslims are a minority in Iran, and it was rumored that some of the Sunni religious leaders were rounded up and executed. Persecution is ongoing. On June 12, 2014, Human Rights Watch reported a controversy over thirty-three Sunni Muslims on death row for "enmity against God."

In 1988, Khomeini issued a death fatwa calling for an act of international terrorism, the assassination of Salman Rushdie and his publishers. Rushdie's so-called crime was writing a novel, *The Satanic Verses*, wherein he ridiculed some aspects of Islam.[13] Khomeini set off a string of death threats, bombings, and mayhem.

According to Iran, the death fatwa against Rushdie is still valid, and since Khomeini is dead, it cannot be rescinded. In 2007, a week after Queen Elizabeth knighted Salman Rushdie, Iran released this statement: "The stance of the Islamic Republic of Iran with regard to this issue has not changed from what was put forward by the Imam Khomeini."[13] In other words, the fatwa is still backed by the Islamic Republic of Iran and Supreme Leader Ayatollah Ali Khamenei.

As for the rest of us, according to a 2007 *Wall Street Journal* article, Iranian Ayatollah Vaez-Tabasi, the head of Imam Reza's shrine, has called for "perpetual holy war."[15]

Atrocities against Muslims by Non-Muslims

Atrocities are committed against Muslims, too. Serbs raped thousands of Bosnian Sunni Muslim women, and Bosnian Muslims were victims of ethnic cleansing. Shiite Hezbollah and Iranian mujahedeen went to protect them.

Muslims are being persecuted in Myanmar. *The New York Times* reported on the herding of people into concentration camps, where they are isolated and denied social services. *Newsweek* reported 100 people were killed and 12,000 forced from their homes.[16]

Albania's Muslims and Christians: A Story of Hope

In contrast, Albania may become the model for Christian and Muslim peaceful coexistence. In Albania, the majority Muslim population helped minority Christians rebuild a church.[17] Albanian Muslims are secular.[18] The percentage of Albanians that attend a religious service once a week or more is only 20%. Fundamentalists consider Albanian Muslims to be apostates at best and infidels at worst.

U.S. Constitution and Fundamentalist Islam: Irreconcilable Differences

According to the Quran, considered by Muslims to be the word of Allah and above man-made laws, "None has the right to be worshipped except Allah." In the United States, citizens have the right to practice any religion, or if they so choose, none at all. The First Amendment to the Constitution of the United States of America is the first of ten amendments known as the Bill of Rights:

> Congress shall make no law respecting an establishment of religion, or prohibiting the free exercise thereof; or abridging the freedom of speech, or of the press, or the right of the people peaceably to assemble, and to petition the Government for a redress of grievances.[19]

Of course, the First Amendment doesn't mean that the United States would countenance the actions of followers of a so-called religion that sacrificed virgins to volcano gods, or tolerate religious hate speech that incites people to commit acts of violence against others.

In the movie, *The Contender,* Joan Allen explains her philosophy as a potential appointee to the position of Vice President of the United States:

> I stand for the separation of Church and State, and the reason that I stand for that is the same reason that I believe our forefathers did. It is not there to protect religion from the grasp of government but to protect our government from the grasp of religious fanaticism.[19]

Yes, it's a movie, but the scriptwriters got it right. The free exercise of religion stops where infringement on the rights of other citizens begins. The Bill of Rights includes the Ninth Amendment, which states: "The enumeration in the Constitution of certain rights shall not be construed to deny or disparage others retained by the people."

For example, Warith Deen Umar ran the New York Islamic prison program for a couple of decades and praised the September 11, 2001 (9/11), hijackers in an article. He also recruited prisoners to radical Islam. After he was banned from the prison system, New York Senator Charles E. Schumer had this to say about free speech with regard to Umar:

> You err on the side of liberty, but you still have to protect yourself. Free speech is not absolute. Free speech is different in different contexts. Incitement has a lower threshold in prison than on, say, a dairy farm.[20]

Fundamentalist Muslims who claim that the United States doesn't have freedom of religion because fundamentalists can't engage in, say, speech to incite imminent violence, are using sophistry. If that is what we meant by the First Amendment, then non-Muslims could start a religion that incites imminent violence against Muslims. Fortunately, neither criminal Muslims nor criminal non-Muslims can hide behind "freedom of religion" to do whatever they please.

Our ideology is stated right at the outset:

> We the People of the United States, in Order to form a more perfect Union, establish Justice, insure domestic Tranquility, provide for the common defense, promote the general Welfare, and secure the Blessings of Liberty to ourselves and our Posterity, do ordain and establish this Constitution of the United States of America.

Muslims are welcome in the United States, but they are bound by our laws and cannot claim sharia laws supersede them.

It seems to me that "Islamophobes" are not the people who speak and write about these issues; rather, Islamophobes are the people who are too frightened by potential fundamentalist Muslim retaliation to engage in an honest discussion.

Just before Islamic scholar and Karachi University professor Dr. Muhammad Shekeel Auj was murdered in September 2014, he advocated capital punishment for terrorists and said extremism leads to persecution: "It spreads and envelops everything around it." Modern Muslims in Pakistan refuse to discuss or debate issues and "want to impose their own will at gunpoint." The professor was gunned down on his way to a reception at Karachi's Iranian Cultural Center.[21]

Calling a belief religion doesn't make it holy, sacred, just, or wholesome. We cannot allow bullies to hide behind the word "religion" and undermine civilization. If our political leaders allow that to happen in the United States, then a new religion may spring up: the Constitutionalists.

Chapter 5

Clash of Civilizations

When the first beginnings of evil which may subsequently challenge peace and freedom and even the life of the state make their appearance on the horizon, it is right then to sound the alarm and try to arouse somnolent authority to novel dangers.

—Winston Churchill

On the morning of February 26, 1993, I walked from the World Trade Center's Twin Towers, through the sky bridge over Liberty Street, to my job in the forty-story New York skyscraper known as One World Financial Center.

At 12:17 pm, the trading floor rumbled and shook. One of my colleagues dove under the desk. Another asked if a gas main had exploded. I suspected a bomb. After news reports confirmed it was a bomb, I immediately wondered if the culprits were Iranian. I was right about the bomb, but I was wrong about the culprits.

Seven members of a terrorist cell were eventually convicted in connection with the attack. They had conspired to bring down the Twin Towers of the World Trade Center with a cyanide-stuffed 1,300-pound urea nitrate-hydrogen gas bomb. They loaded it into a truck, drove onto a ramp in the underground parking lot of the North Tower, and set it off.

The explosion killed six people and injured more than a thousand other innocents. Victims suffered from smoke inhalation as they made their escape down the steps of the skyscraper. But the attempt to explode the North Tower into the South Tower—toppling both and killing tens of thousands—failed.

Ramzi Ahmad Yousef, a Kuwaiti, was the alleged "mastermind" of the 1993 World Trade Center bombing. In 1994, he bombed Philippines Airlines Flight 434, killing a passenger. The pilot managed to safely land the plane, despite a huge hole blown through the side of the hull.

In 1996, Yousef and two other Muslim radicals were convicted of conspiring in "Project Bojinka," a three-part plan to bomb eleven United States jets, kill 4,000 passengers, assassinate Pope John Paul II, and fly a plane into an important U.S. domestic target.[1] According to the 9/11 Commission Report, in 1995, "Ramzi Yousef's accomplice in the Manila airlines bombing plot...told Philippine authorities that he and Yousef had discussed flying a plane into CIA headquarters."[2]

On November 12, 1997, Yousef was convicted of the 1993 World Trade Center bombing in a New York jury trial. He was later sentenced to life in prison.[3] His accomplices included two Palestinians, an Egyptian, a Jordanian, another Kuwaiti, and a U.S.-born citizen raised in Iraq. A blind, Egyptian-born Muslim cleric, who was living in the U.S. when the bombings occurred, is serving a life sentence as a co-conspirator.

Khaled Sheikh Mohammed (KSM), Yousef's maternal uncle, is believed to be a senior operative of al-Qaeda. He confessed under torture to masterminding up to a dozen terrorist attacks, including 9/11 and the 1993 attack on the World Trade Center.[4,5] KSM is currently a resident of either Guantanamo or a CIA black site.

The torture casts a shadow of doubt on KSM's confessions. In September 2014, Senator Dianne Feinstein said the U.S. Senate will publish the Torture Report detailing the treatment of al-Qaeda suspects in U.S. custody.

The investigation into the 1993 World Trade Center bombing has taken more than two decades. As the investigation uncovered suspect after suspect, there wasn't an Iranian among them. Although the terrorists weren't Iranian, they were all fundamentalist Muslims.

Second Time: 9/11

On September 11, 2001, it was already afternoon in London when five hijackers flew American Airlines Flight 11 into the North Tower of the World Trade Center.

Within minutes, my British colleagues and I were riveted to the trading floor's television screens tuned to CNN. We watched in horror as another five hijackers crashed United Airlines Flight 175 into the South Tower.

Some of my friends and former colleagues in New York worked in the burning buildings. I hoped the fires could be controlled, or that my friends either hadn't yet arrived at work or were in the process of evacuating.

Those who fled the North Tower and saved themselves recalled that some of their colleagues didn't leave. Building officials made an announcement over the intercom telling people to stay in their offices. Those who didn't listen survived.[6]

Meanwhile, people in the as-yet undamaged South Tower started down the stairs and heard a similar announcement. Many ignored the fatal advice. The South Tower's stairwell shook and swayed when the second jet hit 18 minutes after the first one crashed into the North Tower. As evacuees continued down the stairwells, they passed firefighters and other emergency responders rushing up towards the fire. Most of those responders didn't survive.

Five hijackers crashed American Airlines Flight 77 into the Pentagon. Six crew members, sixty-four passengers, and 125 people in the Pentagon building were killed.

Four more terrorists hijacked United Airlines Flight 93 intending to crash the plane into the Capitol Building or the White House, but passengers called their friends and families and were told of the World Trade Center disaster. When the passengers fought the Flight 93 hijackers for control, the terrorists intentionally crashed the plane near Shanksville, Pennsylvania.

The 9/11 death toll included almost 3,000 victims: passengers in the four airplanes, people in the World Trade Center, people in the hotel next door, emergency first responders, and military personnel at the Pentagon. Nineteen hijackers were also killed.[7] The remains of bone and tissue fragments are still being matched. Tens of thousands of first responders have ongoing health problems from toxic inhalation and other injuries.

It was horrific, but it could have been even worse. Had the attack occurred later in the morning, tens of thousands of people would have been in the buildings.

Osama bin Laden: Porn and Regret

The 9/11 hijackers were part of the al-Qaeda terrorist network under Osama bin Laden, a

Saudi Arabian from a wealthy family connected to the royal family. Khalid Sheik Mohammed, the mastermind of the attack who confessed under torture, is believed to be a citizen of Kuwait, Bosnia, and Pakistan.[8]

Of the nineteen hijackers, fifteen were citizens of Saudi Arabia, two were from the United Arab Emirates, one was from Lebanon, and one was from Egypt.

Almost ten years after 9/11, Navy Seals, temporarily acting under the authority of the Central Intelligence Agency, executed Operation Neptune Spear. On May 2, 2011, they stormed bin Laden's tacky compound in Abbottabad, Pakistan. The Seals terminated bin Laden's terrorism career with extreme prejudice. They also killed one of his three wives, one of his adult sons, his brother, and one of his couriers.

The Seals buried bin Laden's corpse at sea. President Obama commented on the choice of burial and the decision not to show a photo of the body: "Imagine how the American people would react if Al Qaeda killed one of our troops or military leaders, and put photos of the body on the internet."[9]

I wasn't sure if that was meant as a joke. Al-Qaeda had killed U.S. military leaders in the 9/11 Pentagon attack. The internet was filled with horrific images of desperate people jumping from the World Trade Center's twin towers to escape the fire. Al-Qaeda beheaded people and put videos on the internet. Our reaction was clear; it was Operation Neptune Spear.

Forensic analysts recovered a treasure trove of documents and plans for further terrorism from bin Laden's home.[10] Among other schemes, bin Laden tried to recruit an operative with a valid Mexican passport to illegally cross into the United States at the southern border to conduct terror operations

Analysts also found banned-by-Islam porn on bin Laden's computer. Osama bin Laden's documents revealed him to be a narcissist.[11] After his symbolic attack on capitalism, he was concerned that al-Qaeda wasn't given credit for the economic downturn in the Unites States. He was self-involved and craved notoriety. After his death, many Muslim clerics lionized him, but in the end, bin Laden and his supporters looked pathetic.[12]

It is true that 9/11 was horrific; with its 3,000 fatalities and 30,000 related injuries. But according to the Department of Justice, in 2011, there were 14,610 homicides in the United States. According to the Centers for Disease Control and Prevention, around 600,000 people die of heart disease each year in the United States, partly due to easy living.

The U.S. involved itself in Middle East wars, but bin Laden was about as relevant as a Somali pirate. We invaded Iraq on the pretext of going after the late Saddam Hussein's weapons of mass destruction, and of course, Iraq has oil. We didn't find weapons of mass destruction, and we didn't secure the oil.

In 2003, the U.S. government estimated the Iraq War would cost $50 to $60 billion. As of March 2013, The Costs of War Project at Brown University estimated the Iraq War alone took more than 190,000 lives and cost $2.2 trillion.[13] The combined costs of the wars in Afghanistan, Iraq, and Pakistan cost $4 trillion and more than 330,000 lives.

Bin Laden wanted to damage the U.S. economy, but he didn't make a dent compared to Wall Street executives. The 2008 financial crisis led to the largest no-strings-attached bailout of the banking system in the history of the United States. The following year, the CEO of a bailed out bank—that was sued for fraud by the SEC—responded to concerns about $20 billion he earmarked for bonuses.[14,15] He quipped he was just a banker "doing God's work."[16]

Without producing anything except financial transactions, bankers skim off an outsized portion of gross domestic product (GDP). The financial industry accounted for only 2.8% of GDP in 1950, but in 2012, the financial industry accounted for 7.9% of GDP, representing 30% of corporate profits. GDP growth in the United States is well below historical trend lines, since money for capital investment was diverted to the financial system. As of July 2014, more than 46 million U.S. citizens were on food stamps.

Islamic States and Lust for Global Islamic Domination

Osama bin Laden wasn't as much trouble as he wanted to be, but overall, Islamic terrorism is a looming threat. The U.S. Department of State's list of terrorist organizations shows that most of them are Islamic.[17] The Defense Intelligence Agency estimates there are forty-one Islamic terrorist organizations in twenty-four countries (up from twenty-one in eighteen countries ten years ago), including Hezbollah, HAMAS, the Abu Nidal Organization, al-Qaeda, Army of Islam, ISIS, Islamic Jihad Union, Ansar al Sharia (aka al-Qaeda in the Arabian Peninsula or AQAP), Jabhat al-Nusra, Lashkar-e-Taiba, the Muslim Brotherhood, the Taliban, Al-Islah, Houthis, Harakat Shabaab al-Mujahidin (aka al-Shabaab, Ash-Shabab, Hisbul Shabaab), al-Barakat, Al-Ittihad Al-Islami (AIAI), An-Nusrah, the Mahdi Army in Iraq, Boko Haram,[18] Abu Sayyaf, and more. Al-Qaeda has branches in Yemen, Libya, the Philippines, and India.

The 9/11 terrorists entered the United States through major airports, and cleared immigration using either student visas or phony visas. Yet our biggest vulnerability seems to be our southern border.[19]

In January 2011, Border Patrol agents found Muslim cleric Said Jaziri hiding in the trunk of a BMW. He traveled via Tunisia, Europe, Central

America, and then Mexico (at Chetumal on the Mexico-Belize border). Once in Mexico, he made his way to Tijuana, and then traveled on foot over the border where the BMW awaited. A Tunisian citizen, he was deported from Canada in 2007 for lying about being deported from France, after he assaulted another Muslim who wasn't devout enough for him. Jaziri had also called for the death of the Danish cartoonist who had drawn caricatures of Muhammad.

In April 2011, Somali citizen Ahmed Muhammad Dhakane was convicted in Texas for making false statements while seeking asylum in the United States. He was affiliated with al-Barakat and the AIAI, both on the U.S. Department of the Treasury's Specially Designated Global Terrorist list. Dhakane told U.S. officials he smuggled East Africans and had smuggled or attempted to smuggle AIAI-affiliated Somalis into the United States. He also described three smuggled Somalis—known to be affiliated either with AIAI or al-Shabaab—who were prepared to wage jihad in the United States if conflicts expanded overseas.

Anthony Joseph Tracy smuggled 272 Somalis into the United States via Kenya, Cuba, Belize, and Mexico. Members of al-Shabaab asked for his assistance, but he claimed he declined to help. Investigators, however, were troubled by one of Tracy's emails in which he wrote that some of the Somalis he helped were "bad and i [sic] leave them to ALLAH..."

Meanwhile, Hezbollah is active in Latin America in a region where cocaine smuggling and money laundering help fund Hezbollah activities. Latin America is home of the largest Lebanese population in the world, and Iran courts Latin American leaders.

Iran, Terrorist Plots, and U.S. Retaliation

In October 2011, an undercover agent for the Drug Enforcement Agency, who had infiltrated the Mexican drug and crime syndicate known as Los Zetas, helped foil an Iranian assassination attempt against the Saudi Ambassador to the United States, Adel al-Jubeir.

The U.S. has alleged that Manssor Arbabsiar and Gholam Shakuri conspired to hire the drug ring to blow up a Washington D.C. restaurant, along with the Saudi ambassador and everyone else inside. That got the attention of sleepy Congressmen, since any one of them might have been collateral damage.[20] Supreme Leader Ayatollah Khamenei apparently ordered the attack in retaliation for the United States' support of the attempted ousting of Syria's President Bashar al-Assad.

According to a November 2012 report by the U.S. House Committee on Homeland Security, Subcommittee on Investigations, General Baghbani is a commander of the Quds force "that works closely with Hezbollah in conducting terror operations throughout the world."[21] He worked with the Taliban trafficking opium and heroin from Afghanistan to Iran, to make money to support Hezbollah. Iran has been effective at skirting U.S. sanctions through the Islamic Republic of Iran Shipping Lines, by frequently changing ships' ownership, names, and flags.

Iran cultivated relationships in Latin America via business investments and possibly drug smuggling. It set up eleven embassies in Latin American countries including, Venezuela, Bolivia, Chile, Colombia, Nicaragua and Uruguay. Iran may hope to use Venezuela and Bolivia as sources of uranium.

After the thwarted attempt to set off a bomb in our capital, Congress approved a plan to bring down the Central Bank of Iran. We froze the bank's assets and, along with Europe, we virtually blocked Iran's ability to move money through the global banking system.

It is interesting that while U.S. banks were fined small amounts for money laundering for drug cartels, there were no criminal indictments. Yet Standard Charter paid a $667 million fine for breaching our Iran sanctions and entered into a deferred prosecution agreement for conspiracy to violate the International Emergency Powers Act. John Peace, the bank's chairman, was forced to retract an earlier statement that the violation hadn't been willful; the bank accepted responsibility for "knowing and willful criminal conduct in violating U.S. economic sanctions."[22]

Our sanctions were effective enough to drive Iran into hyperinflation. Then in 2014, instead of using our advantage as leverage for regime change, the Obama administration decided to relax sanctions in exchange for Iran's cooperation on nuclear weapons,

The naiveté of our elected officials is astounding. Contracts don't mean much to Iranians. A signed document is just a prelude to altering terms without notice. In the case of Iran's nuclear program, terms will change as soon as Iran catches the watchdogs napping. We gave up an advantage for nothing. Fortunately for our leaders, we don't impose fines or demand retractions when they put us at risk.

In a 2014 interview with the *Financial Times*, Prince Turki al-Faisal, the former head of Saudi Arabian intelligence, remarked, "America is in an era of choices, yet it seems incapable of making them." He added, "While the wolf is eating the sheep, there is no shepherd to come to the rescue" of the rest of the flock.[23] In this sophisticated game of international deception, the former intelligence officer didn't mention that Saudi Arabia has its own wolf pack and may be a bigger sponsor of international terrorism than Iran.

ISIS and Saudi Arabia: the Arabian Peninsula and Oil

ISIS, the Islamic State of Iraq and Syria, also called the Islamic State of Iraq and the Levant or ISIL, is led by Abu Bakr al-Baghdadi, who now calls himself Caliph Ibrahim. In June 2014, ISIS, then an organization of around 30,000 members, announced the creation of an Islamic state, a caliphate, with authority over the world's 1.6 billion Muslims.

Al-Qaeda had wanted to form a caliphate, but it was waiting to gather more power. In September, Boko Haram in Nigeria, inspired by ISIS, also declared its own caliphate.[24] Caliphate means a successor to Muhammad, and there can be only one, so Boko Haram's declaration is a seed for further conflicts.

In his September 10, 2014, address to the nation, President Barack Obama made the following claim:

> Now let's make two things clear: ISIL is not Islamic. No religion condones the killing of innocents, and the vast majority of ISIL's victims have been Muslim. And ISIL is certainly not a state.[25]

I was reminded of Dr. Richard Feynman's retort to a man who badgered him to create an anti-gravity machine:

> I don't pretend that the laws of physics are different so I can create an anti-gravity machine. The game is to use what I know.

ISIS' ideology has the same roots as Saudi Arabia's, the teachings of Muhammad ibn Abd al-Wahhab.[26] This brand of Islam condones killing of people who are innocents, by my definition. The House of Saud used this ideology as a cudgel in the 18th century when it formed the first Saudi state, and ISIS is following suit.

ISIS used to be a branch of Al-Qaeda in Iraq, before the two terrorist groups severed ties. The U.S. supplied arms and training to the Iraqi military, and now some of them are part of ISIS. Nothing would terrify the governments of the Persian Gulf states more than Sunni terrorist groups uniting under Baghdadi, thereby strengthening his claim to running a caliphate.

Where did ISIS get its funding? One theory is that Saudi Arabia and Qatar helped ISIS get its start by supplying the money.[27] It is just a theory, but it is plausible. Osama bin Laden first formed al-Qaeda in Afghanistan and was financed via the "Golden Chain." According to the 9/11 Report, Osama's mujahedeen were financed through nongovernmental organizations and so-called charities supplied with cash by Islamic states in the Persian Gulf and Saudi Arabia.[28]

In a July 13, 2014, article, *The Independent's* Patrick Cockburn related a conversation between Sir Richard Dearlove, head of MI6, the British Secret Intelligence Service, and Prince Bandar bin Sultan of Saudi Arabia. The Prince explained: "The time is not far off in the Middle East, Richard, when it will be literally 'God help the Shia.' More than a billion Sunnis have simply had enough of them."[29]

That's a bit rich coming from the Saudis given their complaint that if the United States pulled out of Iraq, Shias would engage in a program of ethnic cleansing against the Sunni minority. Is it a coincidence that ISIS Sunnis executed northern Iraq's Shia religious leaders?[30] According to Cockburn, Saudi Arabia played a key role in supporting ISIS' anti-Shia jihad, including the murder of Shiite women and children in Kirkuk and slaughter of Shiite air force cadets in Tikrit.

In northern Iraq, ISIS also targets Alawites (another Muslim sect), Christians, and Yazidis (a pre-Islam religious minority).[31] Beheadings of Christians and Alawites are used as terror tactics to make the local population submit or flee for their lives, but most victims are shot.[32] Hundreds of thousands of Christians fled Syria to escape persecution by ISIS, where, among other things, the terrorists are selling women as slaves.[33,34] Is this ISIS' way of carrying out the Saudi Arabian Wahhabi Grand Mufti's fatwa to destroy churches?

If the Saudis funded ISIS, the strategy is backfiring. ISIS plundered like a godless horde and now has enough assets and oil facilities to be self-sufficient. In August 2014, ISIS controlled enough oil to bring in an estimated $3 million per day.[35] They have invaded land from northern Syria to central Iraq, and they are pushing in all directions, including into Turkey.

Saudi Arabia, Oman, Iraq, Jordan, Kuwait, Bahrain, Qatar and the UAE have offered to help us fight ISIS.[36] Others, including Turkey (currently fighting Kurds who are fighting ISIS) and Syria, may join the opposition.

Why don't we just let them fight it out amongst themselves and mop up afterwards? Are we only intervening because we suspect ISIS—if given a chance to control more territory—won't cooperate when it comes to oil production and sales?

In August 2014, ISIS released a video showing the beheading of an American freelance war correspondent, James Foley, followed by separate September videos of the beheadings of American journalist Steven Sotloff and British captive David Haines.[37] An early October video showed the beheading of British hostage Alan Henning.[38]

Our ally, Saudi Arabia, beheaded thirty-four people from January through the first half of August 2014.[39] Crimes ranged from murder to law-breaking that involved no loss of life: sorcery and smuggling hashish. There's no outcry in the United States about Saudi Arabia's beheadings, because our government views this as Saudi Arabia's internal government business as long as no Westerners are executed.

In the United States, we need motor vehicles, and we need oil to make gasoline to run them. Since oil is globally traded, the price of a marginal barrel of oil is influenced by swing capacity of the low cost producer, and Saudi Arabia sits on a sea of oil that's cheaper to extract than ours. We still import around 13% of our needs from Saudi Arabia. Around 10% of the world's oil supply flows through the Saudi Arabian seaport of Ras Tanura, the largest oil terminal in the world.

Saudi Arabia, through Aramco, produces more oil than any other single country in the world. It produces more than Royal Dutch Shell, Exxon Mobile, British Petroleum, and the National Iranian Oil Company combined. That's why Saudi Arabia has so much clout.

The United States has an interest in protecting Saudi Arabia's assets from terrorist attacks or control by terrorists. I appreciate the economic reasons for not criticizing Islam, and thus the Saudis, but political expediency can go too far.

USA: Infiltration and Resistance

On November 5, 2009, military psychiatrist Major Nidal Malik Hasan shot and killed thirteen people and wounded thirty others at Fort Hood, a military post in Killeen Texas. General Barry McCaffrey opined: "It's starting to appear as if this was a domestic terrorist attack on fellow soldiers by a major in the Army who we educated for six years while he was giving off these vibes of disloyalty to his own force."[40] The United States Department of Defense classified the incident as an act of workplace violence.

Hasan's religious counselor was American-born Imam Anwar al-Awlaki, a suspected al-Qaeda senior operative tied to several acts of terrorism.[41] Al-Awlaki's family moved to Yemen when he was eight. As an adult, he moved back to the United States and was investigated for lying on his social security application; he stated he was born in Yemen, not the United States. In 2000 and 2001, al-Awlaki was imam at a mosque in San Diego, California, and later at a mosque in Falls Church, Virginia. Hasan, the Fort Hood assassin, attended the Virginia mosque as did two of the 9/11 terrorists. A third 9/11 hijacker attended Awlaki's San Diego mosque.[42]

Al-Awlaki posed as a moderate, a virtual ambassador for peace-seeking Muslims, until he moved from the United States back to Yemen in 2004. He used the internet to become the foremost English-speaking proponent of militant Islam and advocated killing innocents, including women and children. On September 30, 2011, al-Awlaki and three other suspected top al-Qaeda operatives were killed in northern Yemen when two Predator drones launched from a secret CIA base destroyed their vehicle with Hellfire missiles.[43]

In October 2010, London-based Muslim cleric Anjem Choudary told Christiane Amanpour on ABC *This Week*, "East and the West will one day be governed by the Sharia. Indeed, we believe that one day, the flag of Islam will fly over the White House;" Muhammad said the "Day of Judgment will not come until a group of my ummah [people of my nation] conquer the White House."[44,45] He also told CNN that he is in communication with people in the United States, and around the world, encouraging them to participate in terrorist attacks, an unambiguous violation of U.S. law.[46] In August 2014, Choudary claimed there's no more ISIS or ISIL; there is only a caliphate. In a nutshell, that is an Islamist's idea of peace.[47]

Scotland Yard arrested Choudary and nine other men in September 2014 on suspicion of terrorism. Choudary was tied to Omar Bakri Mohammad, another hate-speaking Muslim cleric, who was banned from returning to England in 2005. Choudary was also close to Muslim cleric Abu Hamza al-Masri who was found guilty in a New York terror trial in May 2014. Among other illegal activities, al-Masri was trying to found an al-Qaeda training camp in the United States.[48]

Religious philosopher Reverend James Vincent Schall, S.J., who has studied Islamic literature and taught political science at Georgetown University, offered his opinion on why Muslim clerics haven't denounced jihadi violence in a September 2014 essay for *Crisis Magazine*:

> When the original 9/11 happened, there was not condemnation coming from within Islam, but widespread celebration. Islam was seen as winning. But all Muslim scholars know that they cannot, on the basis of the Quran, condemn the use of violence to expand their religion. There is simply too much evidence that this usage is permitted. To deny it would be to undermine the integrity of the Quran.[49]

Muslim terrorist groups are comprised of violent Muslims from multiple cultures and countries. Attacks on the United States included the 1993 World Trade Center bombing, the August 1998 bombing of U.S. embassies in Kenya and Tanzania, the October 2000 bombing of the U.S.S. Cole in Yemen,[50] 9/11, and other myriad global acts of terrorism.[51] The response from the rest of the Islamic world to date has been far too muted. So far the only leader who claims to speak for all 1.6 billion Muslims is the ISIS terrorist, Abu Bakr al-Baghdadi.

The Plan

President Obama has made it clear that he doesn't have a coherent strategy for the Middle East, but Islamic fundamentalists have a plan. That plan is to dominate the Arab homeland and work outward from there, so that the entire globe will hear the daily Muslim call to prayer, and the only flag that will fly will be that of an Islamic caliphate.[52]

ISIS' declaration of a caliphate has reenergized the fundamentalist agenda. This has always been Saudi Arabia's agenda, too, but as far as the younger and meaner extremists are concerned, the Saudis are old, fat, and lazy; they have lost focus and fallen down on the job. Muslim infighting has helped the West by delaying the fundamentalist agenda.

Our response to this agenda has been appeasement to support our oil interests. Meanwhile oil revenues funded extremists.

The global systemic crimes originating from those who practice fundamentalist Islam require a vigorous response from both non-Muslims and enlightened Muslims. Terrorism is spreading and escalating. We haven't yet seen the worst-case scenario, and we're not prepared for it.

We may have little understanding of the fundamentalist Islamic mind, but they also seem to have little understanding of us. Most citizens of the United States came here willingly, not to create havoc, but to build better lives. No matter what our religion, or lack of it, we agreed on a philosophy of government and formed a Republic. Our ancestors often went through great hardship to come here, because they were the kind of people who would not submit. Given the choice between a despot and great inconvenience, they chose, despite suffering and adversity, to hope for freedom and a better future in a new country.

We have the strength to face difficult and complicated truth. Those who claim the United States doesn't have a choice on whether or not to accept sharia law are mistaken. We do have a choice. We made our choice. In this clash of civilizations, we have already chosen the United States Constitution, and we should be prepared to defend it.

You've finished. Before you go...

Tweet/share that you finished this book.

Write a brief customer review on Amazon or your favorite site for book lovers.

Give *Unveiled Threat* as a gift to your favorite Constitutionalist!

Don't miss out! Visit www.janettavakoli.com and sign up for updates on Janet Tavakoli's books.

References

Chapter 1
Iran: The White Revolution

[1]Staff. "Energy Crunch: Real or Phony?" *Time Magazine*, January 21, 1974.

[2]Risen, James. "Secrets of History: The C.I.A. in Iran." *New York Times*, 2000.

[3]Kinzer, Steven. *All the Shah's Men: An American Coup and the Roots of Middle East Terror*. Wiley, 2003.

[4]Sanger, David E. "U.S. Ending a Few of the Sanctions Imposed on Iran." *New York Times*, March 18, 2000.

[5]Byrne, Malcolm (editor). "CIA Confirms Role in 1952 Iran Coup." *The National Security Archive*, August 19, 2013.

[6]Merica, Dan and Hanna, Jason. "In declassified document, CIA acknowledges role in '53 Iran coup." CNN, August 19, 2013.

Chapter 2
Islamic Republic: Descent into Darkness

[1]Follett, Ken. *On Wings of Eagles*. William Morrow & Co., 1983.

[2]Higgins, Andrew. "Inside Iran's Holy Money Machine." *Wall Street Journal*, June 2, 2007.

[3]Harnden, Toby; Hussein, Aqeel; and Freeman, Colin. "Iran 'sponsors assassination' of Sunni pilots who bombed Teheran." *The Telegraph*, October 29, 2005.

Chapter 3
Submission and Resistance

[1]Keneally, Meghan. "Iran passes a law allowing men to marry their 13-year-old adopted daughters just as the country's new president touts himself as a moderate." *Daily Mail (Online)*, October 13, 2013.

[2]Moore, Jack. "Saudi Arabia Drafts Law to Prevent Child Marriage." *International Business Times,* December 18, 2013.

[3]Gardner, Joshua, and Miller, Daniel. "'We are cut off, isolated and alone'; Imprisoned Saudi princesses blame their father King Abdullah as their mother calls on Obama to help free them." *Daily Mail (Online)*, March 27, 2014.

[4]Brown, Stacy. "'We are hostages': A Saudi princess reveals her life of hell." *New York Post*, April 29, 2014.

[5]Staff. "Pope Francis: 'About 2%' of Catholic clergy paedophiles." *BBC News Europe*, July 13, 2014.

[6]Tisdail, Simon. "Seized—for showing their hair." *The Guardian*, May 1, 2007.

[7]BBC. "For arrests over acid attacks against women in Iran." *BBC News* (Middle East), October 20, 2014.

[8]Motevalli, Golnar. “Acid Attacks on Women in Iran Raise Concerns of Veil Vigilantes.” *Bloomberg News*, October 20, 2014.

[9]McVeigh, Tracy. “We don’t want our burqas back: women in Afghanistan on the Taliban’s return.” *The Guardian: The Observer*, January 12, 2013.

[10]Gopal, Anand. “Afghanistan: ‘Jihadis suffocate our voices.’” [Interview of Fatima Nazari, MP] *Inter Press Service News Agency*, March 9, 2009.

[11]Augustine of Hippo. *The City of God*. The Modern Library, 1994.

[12]Lloyd Roberts, Sue. “Demanding justice for women and children abused by Irish nuns.” *BBC News Magazine*, September 23, 2014.

[13]Gupta, Ruchira. “Challenging India’s Rape Culture.” *The Hindu*, January 13, 2013.

[14]Schmitt, Eric. “Military Women Say Complaints of Sex Harassment Go Unheeded.” *New York Times*, March 10, 1994.

[15]Gillibrand, Kirsten. *Off the Sidelines*. Ballantine Books, 2014.

[16]Martosko, David. “‘In these girls, Barack and I see our own daughters’: Michelle Obama demands justice for Boko Haram kidnap girls in White House’s weekly radio address.” *Daily Mail (Online)*, May 9, 2014.

[17]Smith, Alexander. “Nigerian Schoolgirl Kidnapped by Boko Haram found ‘Traumatized.’” *NBC News*, September 26, 2014.

[18]Graham-Harrison, Emma. "Afghanistan still one of the worst places to be a woman, says EU ambassador." *The Guardian*, March 7, 2014.

[19]Jay OBE, Alexis. "Independent Inquiry into Child Sexual Exploitation in Rotherham (1997-2013)." P. 36, *Rotherham Metropolitan Borough Council*, August 21, 2014.

[20]Reid, Sue. "'I was called a liar and a racist for exposing this sex gang abuse horror.'" *Daily Mail (Online)*, August 25, 2014.

[21]Quinn, Ben. "Ex-minister Denis MacShane jailed for bogus expenses claims." *The Guardian*, December 23, 2013.

[22]Infante, Francesca; Robinson, Margin; De Graaf, Mia; McTague, Tom; and Crockhoft, Stef. "'As a true Guardian reader, and liberal leftie, I didn't want to rock the multi-cultural boat' says former Rotherham Labour MP Denis MacShane as he insists no-one raised town's child sex abuse scandal with him." *Daily Mail (Online)*, August 24, 2014.

[23]Seligman Ph.D., Martin E.P. *Learned Optimism*. Vintage, 2006.

[24]Alibhai-Brown, Yasmin. "The truth about Islam and women." *The Independent*, October 1, 2001.

[25]Ignatius, David. "Nobels With a Message." *The Washington Post*, October 14, 2003.

[26]"Interview with Iranian Nobel Prize Winner Shirin Ebadi." *Frontline/World*, November 22, 2003.

[27]"Doctor describes injuries to Canadian woman by Iranian authorities." [report on Zahra Kazemi] CBC News, March 31, 2005.

[28]Saperia, Sheryl, and Ben Taleblu, Behnam. "Opinion: Remembering Zahra Kazemi and continuing rights abuses in Iran." *The Gazette*, July 25, 2014.

[29]Penketh, Anne. "The new suffragettes: Shirin Ebadi—the campaigner who has become an international figurehead for women's rights." *The Independent*, May 30, 2013. [Ebadi finally acknowledges Iran's sharia judiciary is a subsidiary of the Intelligence Ministry.]

[30]Von der Osten-Sacken, Thomas, and Uwer, Thomas. "Is Female Genital Mutilation an Islamic Problem?" *Middle East Quarterly*, Winter 2007, pp 29-36.

[31]Anderson, Lisa. "Female genital mutilation on the rise in the United States—report." *Thomson Reuters Foundation*, March 11, 2013.

[32]Pyati, Archana, and de Palma, Claudia. "Female Genital Mutilation in the United States." *Sanctuary for Families*, 2013.

[33]Staff. "Man gets 10-year sentence for circumcision of 2-year-old daughter." *The Associated Press*, reprinted in *USA Today*, November 1, 2006.

[34]Roberts, Alison. "Ayaan Hirsi Ali: 'FGM was done to me at the age of five. Ten years later, even 20...I would not have testified against my parents." *London Evening Standard*, March 14, 2013.

[35]Hari, Johann. "Ayaan Hirsi Ali: My life under a fatwa." *The Independent*, November 7, 2007.

[36]Van Bakel, Rogier. "'The Trouble Is the West.'" *Reason*, November 2007 issue.

[37]Perez-Pena, and Vega, Tanzina. "Brandeis Cancels Plan to Give Honorary degree to Ayaan Hirsi Ali, a Critic of Islam." *New York Times*, April 8, 2014.

[38]Hodge, Nathan, and Gross, Jenny. "Pakistani Girls' Education Activist Malala Yousafzai Rose to Global Prominence After Taliban Shooting." *Wall Street Journal*, October 10, 2014.

[39]Yousafzai, Malala. *I am Malala: The Girl Who Stood Up for Education and Was Shot by the Taliban*. Little, Brown and Company, 2013.

Chapter 4
Religion of Intolerance

[1]Hitti, Philip Khuri. "*The Arabs: A Short History*." Gateway Editions, October 1, 1996.

[2]"Pakistani Cleric Issues Fatwa Over Cartoons." *Associated Press*, reprinted by *Fox News*, February 17, 2006.

[3]Lavers, Michael K. "Iran a 'paradox' for LGBTs." *Washington Blade*, June 19, 2014.

[4]Barford, Vanessa. "Iran's 'diagnosed transsexuals.'" *BBC News*, February 25, 2008.

[5]Rupar, Terri. "Here are the 10 countries where homosexuality may be punished by death." *The Washington Post*, February 24, 2014.

[6]Toumi, Habib. "Gay man sentenced for Twitter debauchery in Saudi Arabia." *Gulfnews.com*, July 23, 2014.

[7]Simpson, Jack. "Gay Saudi Arabian man sentenced to three years and 450 lashes for meeting men via Twitter. *The Independent*, July 25, 2014.

[8]Heneghan, Tom. "European bishops slam Saudi grand mufti's fatwa against Gulf churches." *Reuters*, March 24, 2012.

[9]"'Islam is Peace' Says President." The White House Archives, September 17, 2001.

[10]"Full text of President Obama's 2014 address to the United Nations General Assembly." *Washington Post*, September 24, 2014.

[11]Religion and Public Life Project, "Mapping the Global Muslim Population." *Pew Research*, October 7, 2009.

[12]Staff. "Destruction of historic Bahai cemetery under way in Shiraz by Iranian Revolutionary Guards." *Bahai World News Service*, May 1, 2014.

[13]Rushdie, Salman. *The Satanic Verses: A Novel*. The Viking Press, 1989.

[14]Staff. "Iran says Rushdie Death Fatwa Still Stands." *Asharq Al-Awsat*, June 24, 2007.

[15]Higgins, 2007.

[16]Ellick, Adam B., and Kristof, Nicholas. "Myanmar's Persecuted Minority." *The New York Times*, June 16, 2014.

[17]Mema, Briseida and Neascu, Calin. "Albania's lesson in Muslim-Christian tolerance." *Arab News*, September 23, 2014.

[18]Khan, Razib. "How religious are Albanian and Bosnian Muslims?" *Discover*, April 16, 2009.

[19]Lurie, Rod, and Allen, Joan. *The Contender*. Film. Directed by Rod Lurie. 2000.

[20]Liptak, Adam. "The Nation: Prisons to Mosques; Hate Speech and the American Way." *New York Times*, January 11, 2004.

[21]Waraich, Omar. "Dr Muhammad Shakeel Auj: Islamic scholar murdered in Pakistan due to his liberal views." *The Independent*, September 24, 2014.

Chapter 5
Clash of Civilizations

[1]CNN staff and Jenkins, Brian, and *Reuters*. "Plane terror suspects convicted on all counts." *CNN*, September 5, 1996.

[2]The 9/11 Commission, Kean, Thomas H., and Hamilton, Lee H., et.al. "Final Report of the National Commission on Terrorist Attacks Upon the United States." July 22, 2004.

[3]Weiser, Benjamin. "Mastermind Gets Life for Bombing of Trade Center." *The New York Times*, January 9, 1998.

[4]Johnston, Ian. "Al-Qaeda suspects were brought to the 'point of death' during 'real torture' by CIA." *The Independent*, September 7, 2014.

[5]CNN Library. "Khalid Sheikh Mohammed [sic] Fast Facts." *CNN*, December 16, 2013.

[6]Newsday. "They didn't listen, and lived." *The Seattle Times*, September 13, 2001.

[7]Staff. "Sept. 11: One Year After." *The Boston Globe*, September 11, 2002.

[8]CNN Library. "September 11th Hijackers Fast Facts." CNN, September 8, 2014.

[9]Kim, Maillie Jane. "Is Obama Right to Not Release the bin Laden Death Photos?" *U.S. News & World Report*, May 4, 2011.

[10]Gardner, Frank and staff. "Osama Bin Laden documents released." *BBC News*, May 3, 2012.

[11]Shane, Scott. "Pornography Is Found in Bin Laden Compound Files, U.S. Officials Say." *The New York Times*, May 13, 2011.

[12]Staff. "Extremists hold Osama bin Laden 'funeral' at U.S. Embassy in London." *Metro*, May 7, 2011.

[13]Brown University. "Iraq War: 190,000 lives, $2.2 trillion." *'Costs of War' Project*, March 14, 2013.

[14]Barofsky, Neil. "Factors Affecting Efforts to Limit Payments to AIG Counterparties [including Goldman Sachs]." SIGTARP-10-003, Office of the Special Inspector General for the Troubled Asset Relief Program, November 17, 2009.

[15]SEC Release 2010-123. "Goldman Sachs to Pay Record $550 Million to Settle SEC Charges Related to Subprime Mortgage CDO." Securities and Exchange Commission, July 15, 2010.

[16]Arlidge, John. "I'm doing 'God's work'. Meet Mr Goldman Sachs." *The Sunday Times,* (*London Times*) November 8, 2009.

[17]Bureau of Counterterrorism. "Foreign Terrorist Organizations." U.S. Department of State, 2014.

[18]Chothia, Farouk. "Who are Nigeria's Boko Haram Islamists?" *BBC,* May 20, 2014.

[19]McCaul, Michael T. (Chairman). "A Line in the Sand: Countering Crime, Violence and Terror at the Southwest Border." A Majority Report by the United States House Committee on Homeland Security Subcommittee on Oversight, Investigations and Management, November 2012.

[20]*U.S. v. Manssor Arbabsiar and Golam Shakuri*; U.S. District Court for the Southern District of New York, Case# 1:11-cr-00897-JFK

[21]McCaul, 2012.

[22]Finch, Gavin, and Mustoe, Howard. "Standard Chartered Forced to Apologize for Iran Statement." *Bloomberg News,* March 21, 2013.

[23]Luce, Edward. "Lunch with the FT: Prince Turki al-Faisal." *Financial Times,* March 14, 2014.

[24]Windrem, Robert. "While World Watches ISIS, Boko Haram Declares Its Own Caliphate in Nigeria." *NBC News,* September 15, 2014.

[25]"Statement by the President on ISIL. " The White House Office of the Press Secretary, September 10, 2014.

[26]Kirkpatrick, David D. "ISIS' Harsh Brand of Islam Is Rooted in Austere Saudi Creed" *The New York Times*, September 24, 2014.

[27]Boghardi, Lori Plotkin. "Saudi Funding of ISIS." *The Washington Institute*, June 23, 2014.

[28]9/11 Commission, 2004.

[29]Cockburn, Patrick. "Iraq Crisis: How Saudi Arabia helped ISIS take over the north of the country." *The Independent*, July 13, 2014.

[30]Hauslohner, Abigail. "Shiite villagers describe 'massacre' in northern Iraq." *The Washington Post*, June 23, 2014.

[31]Jaiabi, Raya. "Who are the Yazidis and why is ISIS hunting them?" *The Guardian*, August 11, 2014.

[32]Staff. "Warning Graphic, Raw Photos—ISIS on Christians: 'There is nothing to give them but the sword.'" *Catholic Online*, August 8, 2014.

[33]*Reuters*. "Christians Flee Syria as Religious Persecution Displaces Millions in 2013." *Newsweek*, July 28, 2014.

[34]Yoon, Sangwon. "Women Herded, Sold to Teens as Prize for Fighting with Islamist Terrorists." *Bloomberg News*, October 2, 2014.

[35]Leigh, Karen. "ISIS Makes Up To $3 Million a Day Selling Oil, Say Analysts." *ABC News*, August 2, 2014.

[36]Black, Ian, and Chulov, Martin. "Arab states offer to help attack ISIS, diplomats say." *The Guardian*, September 14, 2014.

[37]Jalabi, Raya. "David Haines video has marked similarities to Sotloff and Foley killings." *The Guardian*, September 13, 2014.

[38]Loveluck, Louisa, and Samaan, Magdy. "Alan Henning 'was certain he would be freed by Isil captors.'" The Telegraph, October 5, 2014.

[39]Gladstone, Rick. "Saudi Arabia: Executions Draw Rebukes." *New York Times*, August 21, 2014.

[40]CNN. "Investigating Fort Hood Massacre." *Anderson Cooper 360 Degrees*, November 6, 2009.

[41]Johnston, David, and Shane, Scott. "U.S. Knew of Suspect's Tie to Radical Cleric." *New York Times*, November 9, 2009.

[42]Sherwell, Philip, and Spillius, Alex. "Fort Hood shooting: Texas army killer linked to September 11 terrorists." *The Telegraph*, November 7, 2009.

[43]Mazzetti, Mark; Schmitt, Eric; and Worth, Robert F. 'Two-Year Manhunt Led to Killing of Awlaki in Yemen." *New York Times*, September 30, 2011.

[44]Amanpour, Christiane. "Holy War: Should Americans Fear Islam?" *This Week*, ABC, October 3, 2010. Transcript.

[45]Staff Reporter. "Extremist cleric to lead White House protest calling for Muslims to 'rise up and establish Islamic state in America.'" *The Daily Mail,* February 2011.

[46]Spitzer, Eliot and Parker, Katherine. "Terror in the Skies." *Parker Spitzer*, CNN, aired October 29, 2010. Transcript.

[47]Hannity, Sean. "'You are the Enemy of Free People': Watch Hannity's Epic Battle with UK Imam Who Defends ISIS." *Fox News Insider*, Fox News, August 28, 2014.

[48]Jakobsson, Lena. "Jury finds radical Islamic cleric Abu Hamza al-Masri guilty in terror trial." CNN, May 20, 2014.

[49]Schall, S.J., Reverend James Vincent. "It's Time to Take the Islamic State Seriously." *Crisis Magazine*, September 23, 2014.

[50]Perl, Raphael, and O'Rourke, Ronald. "Terrorist Attack on USS Cole: Background and Issues for Congress." *CSS Report for Congress*, The Navy Department Library, January 3, 2001.

[51]The 9/11 Commission. "What to do? A Global Strategy." (Executive Summary) *National Commission on Terrorist Attacks Upon the United States*, July 22, 2004.

[52]Carey, Glen. "Mideast Risks Warlord Era as Jihadists Rise, Nations Fail." *Bloomberg News*, October 3, 2014.

Endnote

The CIA World Factbook is a public resource available for free online.

English translations of Islamic literature, including the Quran and hadiths, are available from all major U.S. bookstores. Some of them have English editions in electronic form that are free downloads.

The Final Report of the National Commission on Terrorist Attacks Upon the United States, the 9/11 Report, is available as a free online resource.

The U.S. Energy Information Administration is a public resource and provides public information on global oil production. The U.S.

Commerce Department provides public data on Gross Domestic Product.

The Constitution of the United States of America is available as a free online resource in English, Arabic, and several other languages. We still mean every word of it.

About the Author

Janet Tavakoli is the founder and president of Tavakoli Structured Finance, Inc., a Chicago-based consulting firm. She is a world-renowned expert on derivative products and securities. Tavakoli is a bestselling author of non-fiction professional finance books and a financial fiction thriller. She is frequently interviewed in *The Wall Street Journal, The Financial Times, New York Times, The Economist, and Bloomberg News*.

For the first time, in *Unveiled Threat: A Personal Experience of Fundamentalist Islam and the Roots of Terrorism*, Tavakoli shares her thoughts on fundamentalist Islam and what it means to the Unites States.

37143915R10088

Made in the USA
Lexington, KY
19 November 2014